Whole Grain Baking

Also by Diana Scesny Greene:

Sunrise, A Breakfast Cookbook, Crossing Press, 1980

Whole Grain Baking

Diana Scesny Greene

THE CROSSING PRESS
Trumansburg, New York 14886

Copyright © 1984 Diana Scesny Greene
Printed in the U.S.A.

Cover by Penknife Studios, Boonton, N.J.
Text designed and typeset by Martha Jean Waters
Inside drawings by Joanne Leary

Library of Congress Cataloging in Publication Data

Greene, Diana Scesny.
  Whole grain baking.

  Includes bibliographical references and index.
  1. Cookery (Cereals) 2. Baking. I. Title.
TX8C8.G74 1984   641.6'31   84-16971
ISBN 0-89594-148-1
ISBN 0-89594-147-3 (pbk.)

Contents

7	Introduction
19	Pastries and Bread
37	Buns and Biscuits
53	Muffins and Quick Breads
53	Crackers and Flat Breads
87	Fritters, Puffs and Pone
97	Griddle Cakes, Unyeasted and Yeasted
109	Blender Pancakes
115	Crepes and Blintzes
123	Granola Snacks and Bars
143	Desserts
181	Index

Introduction

This is a book about baking foods that taste great and are good for you. It is a book about taking the first fruits of the harvest, the whole grains, and turning them into lighter breads and more inviting pastries than you ever imagined possible. The actual techniques are quite simple, but you have to be candid about the odds against you and the counterbalancing rewards. You have learned the techniques of cooking with white flour and white sugar and are probably quite competent with these ingredients. Unfortunately, this gives you little preparation for cooking with whole grains. There is an added difficulty: your family expects to be served the foods it has grown accustomed to.

There's a lot to learn about foods in their natural state; they simply do not behave like processed foods. I have tried to take account of all possible contingencies in my recipes — what to do if your cornmeal is coarse instead of fine, if you have commercially milled rice flour instead of hand milled, if you do not have the right kind of wheat (hard or soft). But to make any sense of my recommendations you need to have a general idea of the range of textures and moisture contents that are possible for flours. When dealing with whole grain flours, flour is no longer simply flour. Storage conditions affect the moisture content, for example, while the heat of high speed milling alters texture. This is the kind of information you can expect to find tucked into chapter introductions and individual recipe instructions.

In order to bake the best product you need to know about your ingredients. You have to be an *active* participant in the process of cooking. Food isn't the by-product of a recipe, a counter full of ingredients and a mixer; there are human elements of design and understanding. There are a specified number of hours spent eating every day. Why look at it as a chore or a mindless task when it can become instead a creative achievement? It will take extra time in the beginning to learn the language of whole grains, to familiarize yourself with the tricks, but after that I doubt you will spend any more time in the kitchen than you do now.

The task is not "How can I get all these health foods past my children and spouse?" but rather "How can I cook something delicious from these new ingredients?"

SHOPPING FOR INGREDIENTS

The importance of using fresh grains, nuts, seeds and flours is critical to the success of your cooking. I can't stress this enough. It means that you must become a careful shopper and question the quality of ingredients you intend to purchase. There is so much rancid food for sale that it is shocking. This is due to government controls and surplus policies that deter farmers and middlemen from putting various crops in the marketplace when they are fresh. As a result, many people are not aware when they are eating rancid foods; they have even developed a taste for them. This was made quite clear to me when a friend asked if I wanted to share the 25 pound sack of roasted peanuts she had just purchased. She made such a point of how delicious they were, that I stopped over for a sample. I could smell something amiss as I brought a handful to my mouth. A few chomps told me the peanuts were very rancid. Clearly, the peanuts would not enhance any recipe and could make someone ill.

At various times we have lived several months outside of Alaska in places where whole wheat breads were available commercially. Opting for convenience, we've tried innumerable brands and always wondered why they usually seemed to lack something in the way of taste. Similarly, whenever I baked goods at my mother's house, buying the flour at the local supermarket, pie crusts and cookies seemed to have a flat flavor. Then I started tasting and smelling the raw flour I was buying and watching open trucks with sacks of flour stand outside of bakeries or in traffic for hours and days in full sun. Then I knew why nothing tasted the way it did at home. Despite the best techniques of bakeries, flour that has been oxidized and stored at hot or even warm temperatures will at best yield mediocre bread, and when the flour is itself devitalized, it devitalizes your body by depleting stores of vitamin E in the process of digesting it.

Nuts and seeds are even more vulnerable to quick oxidation and rancidity. Once they have been shelled their oils begin to oxidize unless the nuts are frozen or kept refrigerated and used within a short period of time. Most nuts do not change in appearance, but you can detect an off odor, somewhat musty. The taste is always conclusive proof of rancidity. Sunflower seeds are easy to spot; fresh ones are a silvery grey and plump. As they age they get dry and off-color, usually yellowing when they are past the point of edibility. Unhulled sesame seeds, in contrast, store amazingly well, though you should check to see that there are no signs of oiliness on the bags they were shipped in.

Milk powders and wheat germ should smell sweet. Cultivate your nose! Natural foods aren't automatically good. If you don't relish the thought of diving into a bag of potato chips that's been opened and sitting on the counter for a month, don't expect cries of delight when you serve the kids a bowl of granola made with stale oats and rancid wheat germ. It isn't going to taste good. There's nothing more disheartening than taking the time and effort to try a new recipe only to have it turn out tasting terrible. Since the publication of *Sunrise* I've worked with hundreds of people who needed only a little practice in purchasing in order to become great cooks.

I've stressed taste more than nutrition so far, since that's our starting point, but you should be aware that rancid fats, whether from nuts, seeds, the germ fraction of grains or extracted oils, cause deficiencies of the B vitamins, A, K and E.[1] They can also cause more serious damage by proliferating the spread of free radicals in the body.[2]

So shop where you know the owners are doing a brisk business in whole grains. Co-ops are good for this reason, in addition to the price breaks they offer. Some of the larger chain stores are putting in extensive health food sections. If the turnover of products is rapid, these stores can be a good source of ingredients at reasonable prices.

---

1. Adelle Davis, *Let's Eat Right To Keep Fit,* pp. 47-48.
2. Durk Pearson and Sandy Shaw, *Life Extension.* The free radical theory of aging is the basis of this excellent book.

COOKWARE

I would like to state at the outset that you should be aware of cookware—especially the capabilities and limits of the pots and pans you are now using.

You have to go heavy gauge for griddles. I had the experience of repeating some of my own recipes, originally tested on soapstone, on a thin Teflon coated griddle. Instant disaster. I became acutely aware of what must have been happening to hundreds of other cooks preparing the same pancakes. Where was the rise, the lightness I had promised? It was in the heat of my inch thick soapstone griddle. I've rewritten most of the recipes so that they will perform reasonably well on any griddle, but bear in mind that life *could* be a lot simpler with the proper cookware. With a heavy griddle, for example, you wouldn't always have to separate the eggs, though I recommend it anyway for truly superior pancakes.

The same rules apply for muffin tins, bread pans and baking stones. My mother called me one Sunday to complain about the bran muffins she had made from my recipe. Oh, they tasted fine, Dad loved them, but could I do something so they'd rise higher? I immediately baked the muffins myself. They rose beautifully. When I investigated her kitchen I found out three things: her muffin tins held very little batter, they were made of thin aluminum, and the oven was not heating to temperature.

Bread pans do a lot for loaves. Depending on the color, gauge and the shine of the metal, you can generate quite a few different characteristics in the bread. These qualities of the metal affect the crispness of the crust, baking time and the degree of vertical rise.

Please find out what's happening in your kitchen and do something about it if you aren't satisfied. Remember, the whole point of baking this way is to produce something better than you've ever had before.

TYPES OF WHOLE WHEAT

Whole wheat flours are not all the same. Get that notion out of your mind entirely. And no matter how many magazine articles you have read telling you that you must use part white flour (albeit unbleached) in your pastries, don't believe it. You can achieve any texture you have ever heard of using *all* whole wheat flour — *provided* it is the right one.

Basically there are two types of wheat — hard and soft. The hard wheats (red winter and red spring) are highest in protein, from 12% to 17% (even higher in the cold northern latitudes). The protein component of wheat is the gluten, and gluten is what traps the air of proliferating yeast cells, so it is essential to use hard wheat in all yeast doughs. Even a yeast dough for a sweet roll will require *hard* wheat. If treated properly, this does *not* translate into hard bread and buns.

For batters relying on baking powder and baking soda (quick risers), hard wheat is generally inappropriate. In this case, the gluten tends to make things tough instead of tender, and the flavor of hard wheat is too distinctive.

Soft wheat, on the other hand, is low in protein, 8% to 10%. It is generally available as soft red pastry wheat and soft white pastry wheat, simply because the flours milled from the respective grains are so colored. If you can get soft white wheat, it is preferable to red, since it bakes up just like refined flour does, in color and consistency, and has a very mild flavor. It is almost impossible to guess you are eating a whole grain flour when soft white wheat is used. However, the flour usually stocked in stores as pastry wheat is soft red. This is good enough reason to get soft white berries and grind your own flour. Should you accidentally use a soft wheat, red or white, in your yeast bread dough, you will get a very crumbly loaf. Should you use it for pancakes or pie crust, the result will be heaven. The relative lack of gluten does not hamper the expanding gases of leavening agents other than yeast. If you haven't used it, believe me, there is no substitute. Soft wheat is delectable — I use it in almost every recipe that does not use yeast.

After you have used the correct flour called for in a recipe, the only place you can still go wrong is in gauging the moisture content of the flour. I have retested these recipes in various locations and found that whole wheat berries as well as the flour ground from them tend to pick up moisture unless stored under stable conditions. If a dough or batter seems too sticky to you, your flour probably has a higher moisture content than any of the flours I have used. This is one of the hazards of cooking with whole grains, but I hope you will agree that a little adjustment of the flour/liquid ratio now and then will be well worth the effort in terms of great taste and good health.

DRY VERSUS FRESH MILK

In response to my food columns in newspapers, I've often been asked why so many recipes specify powdered milk instead of fresh liquid milk. My original intent in writing the cookbook was to devise recipes that could be put together from ingredients that any well-stocked natural foods kitchen would be likely to have. Since I was living in Alaska, fresh milk wasn't one of the ingredients readily on hand. (When it *was* flown in, at five dollars a half gallon, the last thing I did was *cook* with it.) When my neighbor started selling goat milk I was elated, and quickly substituted it for the water and milk powder. Disaster ensued. The pancakes didn't taste the same, and the fluid portion of whole milk just wasn't the same proportion as what I had put together using milk powder and water. I began to understand why non-instant milk powder is the commercial baker's choice. As an unintentional side benefit, I also discovered that non-instant milk powder, when combined with whole wheat pastry flour in particular, gave the pancakes a texture very close to what I remembered white flour used to have. Now, even when fresh milk is available, I still prefer to use non-instant milk powder for stack pancakes.

Nutritionally, non-instant milk powder is superior to instant. It is spray dried at a low temperature, preserving more nutrients and doing less damage to the milk protein. Instant milk powder, on the other hand, has been subject to intense heat in the "instantizing" process, which, while making it taste sweeter, devalues its nutritional components.

When adding non-instant milk powder to a recipe, always mix it in with the dry ingredients (flours), in contrast to instant milk powder, which should be mixed in with the liquids. I still use instant milk in some recipes, however, where the sweetness of instant imparts a flavor I can't achieve using non-instant. To reconstitute non-instant milk powder, use a blender or a whisk and a quick strong arm.

On a cup for cup basis, the two milk powders compare as follows (USDA Agriculture Handbook No. 456, Nutritive Value of American Foods.)

	Dry Non-fat, Non-Instant Milk Powder (1/4 c. powder to 1 c. water)	Non-fat Instant Milk Powder (1/3 c. powder to 1 c. water)
Protein (g)	43.1	24.3
Fat (g)	1.0	.5
Carbohydrate (g)	62.8	35.1
Calcium (mg)	1570.0	879.0
Phosphorus (mg)	1219.0	683.0
Iron (mg)	.7	.4
Sodium (mg)	638.0	358.0
Potassium	2094.0	1173.0
Vitamin A (IU)	40.0	20.0
Thiamin (mg)	.42	.24
Riboflavin (mg)	2.16	1.21
Niacin (mg)	1.1	.6
Vitamin C (mg)	8.0	5.0

I have seen various suggestions for reconstituting non-instant non-fat milk, ranging from 2/3 c. powder per quart to 1 c. powder per quart. While the 2/3 c. measure would yield a milk equal in nutritive value to reconstituted instant milk powder (1 1/3 c. powder per quart water) it tastes rather thin, and is also inconvenient to measure for quantities less than 1 quart. By using 1/4 c. non-instant per cup of water, you'll have a convenient guide for cooking and a delicious milk for drinking.

OIL VERSUS BUTTER

In general, fats are important for the maintenance of overall body health, in particular for the well-being of the nerves, brain, hormonal system and digestive tract. High protein and high fiber are not enough for good health. Three essential fatty acids must be supplied: linoleic, linolenic and arachidonic acids. Linoleic, which is supplied by vegetable oils, nuts and seeds, is absolutely vital and is needed for the absorption of vitamins A, D, E, and K.[1]

Reacting in response to the cholesterol theory of heart disease, the press and many well-intentioned health food enthusiasts have recommended the increased use of polyunsaturates and the decrease of saturated fats in the diet. This has led to a proliferation of highly refined vegetable and seed oils and a wide array of margarine products. After years of research testing this theory, however, it appears that excess polyunsaturates (by excess, I mean in excess of saturated fats) not only do not confer any benefits on cardiac health—they may actually be harmful. They have been shown to cause tumors, increased heart disease, cancer, and mutations.[2]

There are several reasons for the deleterious effects of cooking with oils. While fresh raw oil does confer all the benefits to health mentioned above (to nerves, brain, hormonal system and digestive tract), once it is heated, oil is changed chemically to a form (*cis*—to *trans*—) that has virtually opposite effects. I'm not talking only about the high heat of deep frying. In a study by E.A. Pinkney in 1971 it was discovered that "heating an unsaturated oil (especially corn oil) to 200° for 15 minutes (far less than normal cooking temperatures and time) actually enhances atherosclerosis in animals."[3] Unless you are able to buy raw expeller pressed oils, most of the oils in the supermarket have already been heated to 330° to 380°F. for 12 hours to deodorize them.[4] Finally, oils are extremely susceptible to oxidation in the body, and unless you are well fortified with antioxidants such as vitamins C and E and selenium, excess peroxidized fats produce excess free radicals, which are a contributing cause of cardiovascular disease, cancer and aging.[5]

Contrary to popular belief, margarine does not solve the problem. Never substitute it for butter, which has never been proven to be causative in heart disease when the diet is otherwise adequate. In order to make naturally liquid oils solid, hydrogen is added, thus partially saturating the originally unsaturated fat. All the dangers inherent in the heated liquid oils apply to margarine used in cooking.

Now for the reasons for using butter particularly in granola recipes. Naturally saturated fats such as butter contain cholesterol. Contrary to what oil producers would have you believe, cholesterol is necessary for the production of vitamin D, hormones and bile salts.[6] It is also present in large quantity in the nerves and brain. Its use in cooking does not promote arterial plaque, nor does its oxidation result in free radicals. In view of studies done on the effect of vitamin C and lecithin in preventing cholesterol deposits by keeping cholesterol in suspension in the blood stream and circulating its way out of the body, it appears that a reasonable intake of cholesterol is beneficial to health, especially when balanced by lecithin and vitamin C.[7]

As long as you include whole nuts and seeds in the diet, eat as many fresh and unrefined foods as possible, and make mayonnaise and salad dressings from fresh untreated oils, you will be certain to include enough unsaturated fatty acids in your diet without adding oil by the cupful to cooked foods. If you are unconvinced of the perils of cooking oil and decide to use it nevertheless, at least use it for only ½ the total volume of fats in any given recipe and be as careful as possible in finding a fresh raw oil for all cooking purposes.

Dieters who are tempted to shun fats for caloric reasons should be aware that when fats are undersupplied the body converts sugar to fat faster than normal. Avoiding all fats actually adds to the weight problem. Similarly, small portions of high fiber foods antagonizes the problem. The greater the quantity of bran, the less calories the body will be converting to fat. Wheat bran, in particular, will help the body maintain and regulate its proper weight.[8]

---

1. Adelle Davis, *Let's Eat Right To Keep Fit*, pp. 42-49.
2. Richard Passwater, *Super-Nutrition for Healthy Hearts*, pp. 82-88.
3. Wilfrid E. Shute, *Vitamin E Book*, p. 226.
4. Passwater, *Ibid.*, p. 88.
5. *Ibid.*, pp. 83-88. For the most thorough discussion of the free radical theory of aging and disease, see Durk Pearson and Sandy Shaw, *Life Extension*.
6. Adelle Davis, *Let's Eat Right To Keep Fit*, pp. 115-121.
7. Linus Pauling, *Vitamin C The Common Cold and the Flu*, pp. 191-192.
8. See Ruben's *The High Fiber Diet*.

GRAIN MILLS

Most whole grain flours are now available through health food stores, co-ops and wholesale distributors of natural foods. There are several drawbacks to such commercially milled flours. When flours are steel ground in large quantity and at high speed, the temperatures produced in milling cause a deterioration of the heat sensitive vitamins, particularly of the B group. Both steel and stone ground flours are also susceptible to the same nutritional losses due to the time that elapses between milling, packaging and marketing. The germ particles, whether of wheat, corn or oats, begin to oxidize upon contact with the air, and the longer it takes to get the flour from the mill to the table, the greater are the chances for the germ to go rancid.

The advantages of owning your own grain mill are numerous. Grains and legumes may be purchased in bulk and stored whole. If cool and free of moisture, they will keep almost indefinitely in this state. Flours can then be ground upon demand. I also grind ahead and freeze enough hard wheat flour to make one batch of bread and enough pastry wheat flour for several batches of pancakes in case the temperature drops to -50 and I can't get to the grain mill. Each breakfast cook will have her/his separate reason for keeping a small reserve of ground flour, but be sure these flours are kept under refrigeration or frozen to preserve nutrients.

Flour milling should be a joy, not an ordeal. The simplest and most versatile mill is the Corona steel mill. It is inexpensive, hand operated, and will grind everything from hard wheat flour to peanut butter. Further, it can be cleaned. While I have another larger steel mill, a Diamant, for quantity milling, the Corona is indispensable for a quick cup of corn meal, rice flour or whole bean soy. The grain must be run through the mill several times, and this repeat process, during which the steel plates are brought closer together, makes it easy to obtain the optimum texture for every cooking purpose. Two passes for soft wheat produce a fine pastry flour, while three for hard wheat yield quality bread flour. However, hand operated steel mills are undeniably work and they rarely produce the quantities of flour in the times stated in their manuals. I do not have electricity and happen to enjoy the exercise of grinding grain and the satisfaction gained from maximum involvement with the foods I prepare and serve. If you have neither the time nor the inclination to turn a steel wheel, by all means buy an electric mill. In this case, you may want to consider stones.

Stone mills produce extremely fine flour in one pass. Since most are motor driven, they are effortless and turn out large quantities in minutes. Yeast doughs made from stone ground wheat are remarkably light. With the exception of the Marathon Mill, however, stone wheels cannot be used with oily foods, such as soybeans, peanuts or sunflower seeds. There are also milling stones on the market that slough off annoying amounts of grit, so investigate the model and manufacturer thoroughly. Should you choose a stone mill, the Corona would be a good back up mill for cracked grains and oily seeds and beans.

Pastries and Breads

I bake all of our bread, rolls, crackers, tortilla shells and pastries and have done so for ten years. Please trust me when I urge you to follow the delayed kneading technique outlined in almost all of the recipes for yeasted doughs.

I wish I could claim authorship for this technique, but that belongs to a friend of mine, Betty Borg, whose love of bread is inversely proportional to her love of kneading. When I was first drawing up recipes she was a primary tester. Since she also bakes a large quantity of yeast bread, there was always dough rising at her house. However, in all the times I wandered over to her place, I never caught her in the act of kneading the dough. What I did find her doing was scraping the dough down periodically and giving it a brief series of tucks with a rubber spatula or her hands. One day I simply asked if she had already kneaded the dough or if she was going to do so in another half hour. She grinned and then confessed: by scraping and punching down the dough every half hour for a period of an hour and a half she had been getting very light baked results with only a brief (2 to 3 minute) kneading before the final rise.

Normally, bread recipes require that you knead the dough right after mixing. This is all right for bleached white flour, since it absorbs moisture to total capacity almost immediately. It does not work for whole grain flour, not only because it is coarse, but primarily because it contains particles of bran which take a long time to absorb water and soften. If you knead the dough right after mixing, you will inevitably have to knead in a substantial amount of additional whole wheat flour to manage it, and this will be too much once the bran starts taking up water. Result: heavy and/or crumbly bread. By delaying the kneading for as long as possible (without overproofing, of course), you give the bran and endosperm particles enough time to absorb moisture and swell. At the end of 90 minutes you also will have manipulated the dough enough to build up a fairly extensive gluten network, so that only a minimum amount of kneading with a minimal amount of additional flour will be necessary. Result: soft, moist, springy whole wheat bread.

Basic Sweet Whole Wheat Yeast Dough

At last, 100% whole wheat yeast dough with a bounce — moist light rolls and buns that can be cut, rolled, twisted and filled to anyone's preference. It is rich in egg and butter, while milk solids complement the wheat protein.

1/2 c. lukewarm water
1 tsp. honey
2 T. dry active yeast
1 c. warm water
1/2 c. melted unsalted butter
1/3 to 1/2 c. honey
1 tsp. salt
1/3 c. powdered instant non-fat milk
2 eggs
5 c. whole wheat flour (hard)

1. In a small bowl, measure and stir lukewarm water and honey. Sprinkle the yeast on top and let stand 10 minutes while preparing other ingredients. At the end of 10 minutes, the yeast will be foamy (or proofed), so be sure that the bowl is not too small.
2. In a medium-sized pot, warm the cup of water, butter, honey, salt and milk powder until the butter is melted and the honey dissolved. Cool to lukewarm.
3. In a separate bowl, beat the eggs. Add them to the yeast.
4. Combine the two liquids.
5. Stir the flour into the liquid ingredients using circular strokes until thoroughly combined. The dough will be very soft. See the following pages for instructions on kneading, shaping and baking the dough.

Yield: 24 rolls

THE DELAYED KNEADING TECHNIQUE

The following steps apply to all yeast doughs that call for the delayed kneading technique:

1. Let the dough rest in the bowl for 30 minutes. Stir down and cover with a clean tea towel.
2. Let the dough rise 30 minutes in a warm spot. It should be starting to firm up at the end of this time, so use an oiled rubber spatula or oiled palms to push it down.
3. Let the dough rise, covered, another 30 minutes. Punch down and turn out onto a floured surface. Formica or marble counters or tupperware rolling sheets do not rob moisture from the dough the way wood does and require less additional flour for kneading.
4. Knead the dough for 2 to 5 minutes, incorporating as little flour as possible. If you brush melted butter on the kneading surface instead of dusting it with flour, you'll find the dough kneads much easier.
5. Transfer the dough ball to a buttered bowl (the mixing bowl is fine) and let it rise, covered, in a warm spot for 45 minutes. It should be doubled by this time. Punch down, transfer to a board or counter, and let it rest 10 minutes while you butter the trays or pans.
6. Shape the dough into rolls and let rise 30 minutes. Preheat the oven to 350°F during the last 15 minutes of rising and bake the rolls for 18 to 20 minutes. They should sound hollow when tapped on the bottom. Transfer to wire racks to cool before storing.

SHAPING THE DOUGH

Cut Buns
Simply cut the dough up into 24 pieces with a serrated knife and place them evenly spaced on one large buttered cookie tray (approximately 14 x 16 inches) or two small, round, buttered cake pans (8 inches in diameter).

Crescents
These can be formed by cutting the dough into thirds, rolling each third into a circle 1/4 inch thick, then cutting the circular dough into 8 triangular pieces, as for pie. Roll each wedge from the base of the triangle to the apex, curving the roll into a crescent as you place it on the cookie tray.

Clover Leaves
These take a bit more time to shape but are very attractive. Cut as for cut buns, then pinch each piece of dough into three smaller pieces. Form each of these small thirds into round balls and place three in each of 24 buttered muffin tins.

Round Rolls
These are formed simply by cutting as for cut buns and shaping each dough piece into a round ball and flattening slightly with the palm of the hand as it is placed on the buttered cookie tray.

―――――――――――VARIATIONS―――――――――――

Maple Pecan Snails

    1 recipe Basic Sweet Whole Wheat Yeast Dough
    1/2 c. honey
    1 tsp. cinnamon
    2 c. coarsely chopped raw pecans
    1 c. maple syrup

1. Add 1/2 cup honey and cinnamon to Basic Sweet Dough Recipe at step 2. Let rise according to Delayed Kneading Technique.
2. Divide the dough into three equal pieces. Let rest while preparing the maple pecan syrup.
3. In a medium saucepan, simmer the maple syrup until it turns cloudy, then add the pecans and continue stirring well until the syrup begins to foam. Remove from the heat and cool. It should thicken as it cools.
4. Roll each section of dough into a rectangle approximately 16 x 5 inches. Spread each with one third of the maple pecan mixture.
5. Roll, starting with the longest side of the rectangle, then slice each roll into 8 pieces.
6. Place the snails about an inch apart on well buttered pans and let rise until double, about 25 to 30 minutes.
7. Bake for 18 to 20 minutes at 350°F. (Use the longer cooking time if the snails are close together.) Remove from pans while still warm.

Yield: 24 snails

NOTE: Maple syrup varies in consistency. If the syrup you use is thin, boil it longer before you add the pecans.

24 Pastries and Bread

Bubble Ring

It's fun to pull this ring apart while it is warm. Left over it slices well and is delicious toasted or in French Toast.

1 recipe Basic Sweet Whole Wheat Yeast Dough using 1/2 cup honey.
1 tsp. cinnamon
1/4 c. melted butter
1/4 c. maple syrup
2 c. chopped walnuts or almonds

1. Add cinnamon to Basic Sweet Dough at step 2.
2. Combine melted butter and syrup.
3. Have ready two dishes — one with the melted butter and syrup, the other with chopped nuts.
4. Generously butter an angel food cake pan.
5. Pinch off small balls of dough, dip each in the butter/syrup, then in the chopped nuts. Arrange the coated balls in layers in the tube pan.
6. Press the ring slightly, let rise until almost doubled, about 30 to 40 minutes, then bake 50 minutes at 350°F. Invert immediately. Tap the bottom — it should sound hollow if done.

Yield: 1 large ring — a 10 inch tube or angel cake pan or 2 medium loaves

Stollen

This is our traditional Christmas bread.

> 1 recipe Basic Sweet Whole Wheat Yeast Dough
> 1 tsp. grated lemon or orange rind
> 1 1/2 c. almonds, chopped
> 1 1/4 c. golden raisins
> 1/2 c. chopped honeyed papaya (or other honey preserved fruit)

1. When preparing the Basic Yeast Dough stir the citrus rind into the yeast mixture along with the eggs.
2. Stir in the fruit and nuts last, after the addition of flour.
3. After the final rising, cut the dough in half with a serrated knife, then cut each half into 5 pieces. You will be forming 2 braids.
4. Roll each piece into a 16-inch coil. Braid three coils, joining the three strands of dough together well at the beginning and end of the braid. Then twist two coils and place on top of the braid. Again, pinch the ends of the dough together well and pinch the top twist into the three strand braid at intervals.
5. Transfer to a buttered cookie sheet. Repeat for the second braid. Two braids will fit side by side, crosswise, on a large cookie sheet. Cover with a clean towel and let rise until double, about 30 to 40 minutes. Brush each braid with melted butter and bake 35 minutes at 350°F.
6. You may wish to brush the braids again with melted butter upon removing them from the oven for a softer crust and then sprinkle them with maple sugar, but they will be delicious without either addition. Cool before cutting into thin slices.

Yield: 2 braided loaves

Raisin Cinnamon Buns

Prepare Basic Sweet Whole Wheat Yeast Dough, adding 1 tsp. cinnamon at step 2 and 1 cup dark raisins after the addition of the flour. Raise and knead according to the Delayed Kneading Technique.

Fruit Kolaches

Prepare the Basic Sweet Whole Wheat Yeast Dough, increasing the honey to 1/2 cup. Divide the dough into thirds and roll each into a rectangle approximately 12 x 6 inches. Cut each rectangle into 8 squares and place 2 level tablespoons of apple butter or any other thick sweetened fruit puree in the center of each square. Join the opposite ends of each square at the center, over the filling, to form an envelope of dough. Transfer each "wrapped" bun to a buttered baking pan or buttered stainless cookie sheet. Let rise until double, about 30 minutes. Brush with melted butter and bake for 18 to 22 minutes at 350°F.

Any dried fruit can be used. Simply simmer the fruit in a minimum of water until soft and the liquid evaporated. The idea is to steam the fruit rather than boil it — the dough will not be able to hold the filling if there is any excess liquid.

Yield: 24 kolaches

Cheese Kolaches

Cheese makes another delicious kolache filling. Sweeten kefir cheese, dry sieved cottage cheese or pot cheese with honey, nutmeg, and enough beaten egg to bind. Fill each square with 1-2 T. filling and fold as above.

Whole Wheat Bread

This is the one for sandwiches, French toast and burger buns. It's right for slicing, toasting and grilling savory sandwiches.

    1/2 c. warm water
    1 T. honey
    1 T. dry active yeast
    1 tsp. salt
    3 T. honey
    1/4 c. melted butter
    2 c. hot water
    2/3 c. powdered instant non-fat milk
    6 1/2 c. whole wheat flour (hard)

1. Pour the warm water into a small bowl. Stir in one tablespoon of the honey. Sprinkle the yeast on top and let proof for 10 minutes, until foamy.
2. In a medium-sized bowl, place the salt, remaining honey, butter and hot water (hot enough to melt the butter). When it cools to lukewarm, stir in the instant milk.
3. Add the yeast to the liquid ingredients.
4. Vigorously stir in the flour. The dough should be fairly stiff. Let it rest, covered, for 30 minutes.
5. Stir down the dough, cover, and let rest another 30 minutes.
6. Stir down again, really scraping down the edges with a plastic or rubber spatula (a French spatula works great for this purpose), then recover. Let rest and rise 30 minutes more.
7. Turn out the dough and knead for 3 to 5 minutes, butter the mixing bowl and return the dough ball to it. Cover and let rise in a warm spot until double, about 45 minutes.
8. Punch down and form into 2 loaves. Place in buttered loaf pans and let rise until almost double, about 30 minutes.
9. Bake the loaves about 35 minutes at 375°F. Remove from pans immediately, tapping the bottoms to check that they sound hollow.

Yield: 2 loaves

28   Pastries and Bread

---VARIATIONS---

Rye, Oat, Buckwheat, Triticale, Barley or Corn Bread

Substitute up to 1 cup of any of these flours (or a combination of them) for the same amount of whole wheat flour in the original Whole Wheat Bread recipe. Instead of honey, try sorghum or molasses with the stronger flavored flours such as rye or buckwheat.

Raisin Bread

Cut the dough in half and roll out each half into a rectangle, about 12 x 8 inches. Sprinkle with cinnamon and raisins, then roll, starting with the short side of each rectangle. Be sure to roll tightly to avoid air pockets in the finished loaf. Bake in buttered bread pans as above.

Pecan Bread

Add up to 2 cups chopped pecans or other nuts to the dough after stirring in the flour. Raise and knead as above. Makes especially delicious French toast.

Challah

Yellow from the yolks of fresh eggs, this makes attractive and clean slicing loaves for sandwiches and toast.

    1 1/3 c. lukewarm milk*
    1 T. honey
    2 T. dry active yeast
    3/4 tsp. salt
    1/4 c. honey
    1/4 c. melted butter
    3 beaten eggs
    5 1/4 c. whole wheat flour (hard)

1. Pour the warm milk into a medium bowl and stir in the honey until dissolved. Sprinkle the yeast on top and let proof in a warm spot for 10 minutes, until foamy.
2. Whisk in the salt, the remaining honey, butter and eggs.
3. Vigorously stir in the whole wheat flour.
4. Let rest and rise as for Whole Wheat Bread, giving the dough up to 1 hour on the final rise.
5. To shape, cut the dough into 6 sections. Roll each into a thick rope slightly longer than the length of your bread pan. Braid 3 ropes of dough per loaf.
6. Place the braids in buttered pans and let rise until almost double, between 45 minutes and an hour.
7. Bake 35 minutes at 375°F. Remove from pans immediately and cool on wire racks.

Yield: 2 loaves (or 16 braided buns)

---

*You may substitute 1 1/3 cups lukewarm water plus a rounded 1/3 cup powdered instant non-fat milk for the fluid milk.

English Muffins

A top of the stove bread. Cool thoroughly before splitting with a fork and toasting.

This is one case where the delayed kneading technique doesn't apply. The unique texture of English muffins requires a process all its own.

1/2 c. lukewarm water
1 T. dry active yeast
1 c. hot water
2 tsp. honey
3 T. butter
3/4 tsp. salt
2 c. whole wheat flour (hard)
1 3/4 to 2 c. additional whole wheat flour (hard)
1/4 c. non-instant non-fat milk powder

1. Measure the lukewarm water into a small bowl. Sprinkle the yeast over it and let proof for 10 minutes, until foamy.
2. Meanwhile, combine the hot water, honey, butter and salt in a medium bowl. (The butter should melt in the hot water.) Cool to lukewarm.
3. Whisk together about 2 cups flour and the milk powder.
4. Add the yeast solution to the melted liquids, then whisk in the flour/milk powder mixture. At this stage the dough is a "sponge." Cover and let rise for about 1 1/2 hours, until it has at least doubled in volume or threatens to run over a medium sized bowl.
5. Stir in the melted butter and 1 3/4 to 2 cups additional flour. The dough should be quite stiff. If it looks like you'll have a hard time handling the dough after 30 minutes, add another fourth cup flour *now*.
6. Cover and let rest 30 minutes.
7. Turn out the dough and knead a full 10 minutes, adding the least possible amount of flour to work the dough.
8. Roll to 1/2 inch thickness and cut out into 3 inch rounds with a sharp pastry cutter. It is essential to have the edges sharp so that you make a clean straight cut. If the muffin is pinched it won't rise in proper English muffin form.

9. Place as many of the rounds as you can fit on a cold buttered griddle or heavy frying pan and let rise until doubled, about 30 minutes. Place the others on a surface dusted with cornmeal or whole wheat flour.
10. Place the griddle or frying pan over medium to high heat, depending on the gauge of the utensil, then bake the muffins for 6 minutes over moderate heat on the first side. Turn and cook for 4 minutes on the second side. The object here is to heat the griddle quickly once the muffins have risen, but only to the point of transferring slow to moderate heat to the muffins.

Yield: 12 (3-inch) muffins

Pastries and Bread

Whole Wheat Bagels

These light, chewy bagels without gluten flour are a whole grain adaptation of Jean Kaufman's excellent recipe. They are a treat warm with butter and cream cheese or split and broiled with melted cheddar. Like English muffins, bagels require a special technique of raising.

>   1 tsp. honey
>   1/3 c. lukewarm water
>   1 T. dry active yeast
>   2/3 c. hot water
>   2 T. honey
>   3/4 tsp. salt
>   3 T. butter
>   1 egg plus 1 yolk, beaten
>   3 1/2 c. whole wheat flour (hard)
>   (1 egg yolk + 1 tsp. cold water, as a wash
>   before baking)

1. In a small bowl, dissolve one teaspoon honey in lukewarm water. Sprinkle the yeast on top and let proof for 10 minutes, until foamy.
2. Meanwhile, measure into a medium bowl the hot water, two tablespoons honey, salt and butter. (The water should be hot enough to melt the butter.) Cool to lukewarm.
3. Add the beaten egg plus yolk to the yeast, then add this mixture to the honey/salt/butter mixture.
4. Stir in the flour. Cover and let rest for 30 minutes.
5. Turn out the dough and knead for 5 minutes. Butter the mixing bowl, return the dough to it and cover.
6. Let the dough rise until double, about 1 hour, then punch down.
7. Cover and let rise another 45 minutes, then punch down.
8. Repeat step 7.
9. Cut the dough into 12 equal pieces. Roll each into a rope just long enough to overlap when joined into a ring around two fingers. Seal the joint well by rolling the bagel between your fingers and the kneading or cutting board.

10. Have ready 2 quarts boiling water. Add 1 T. honey. Drop the bagels into the boiling water, 4 at a time, and turn them over, starting with the first bagel, as soon as the last bagel has been dropped in the water.
11. Cook 1 minute from the time the last bagel is turned over.
12. With a slotted spoon or spatula, transfer the bagels to a buttered cookie sheet and bake at 375°F. for 20 minutes.
13. For a golden glaze, brush on an egg wash (1 egg yolk beaten with 1 tsp. cold water) before baking.

Yield: 12 bagels

Pumpernickel

I cannot urge you strongly enough to buy a baking stone for your oven if you do not already own one. I use a "super stone," which is a 12 inch stoneware round. It is indispensible for baking free form loaves, such as pumpernickel, so that they look the way they do coming from a bakery. I have tried cookie sheets of every metal and alloy on the market, and none provide the penetrating heat necessary to make a loaf jump straight up once it contacts the pre-heated stone. You eliminate the problem of free form loaves spreading out during baking if you use a stone.

Potato water adds starch, which gives pumpernickel its unique texture.

> 3 medium potatoes
> 4 c. water
> 1 T. dry active yeast
> 1/2 c. lukewarm water
> 2 T. melted butter
> 1/3 c. molasses
> 1 tsp. salt
> 1 1/2 T. caraway seeds
> 5 c. whole wheat flour (hard)
> 3 c. rye flour

1. Boil 3 medium-sized baking potatoes, scrubbed and quartered, in 4 cups water until the potatoes are soft. Remove the potatoes and cool the liquid to lukewarm. You will need 2 1/2 cups of warm potato water. (You can also use leftover potato cooking water; in that case, just heat to lukewarm.)
2. Sprinkle the yeast over the half cup lukewarm water and let proof for 10 minutes. If you have extra potato water, use it instead of plain water.
3. While the yeast is proofing, combine in a medium bowl the warm potato water, butter, molasses, salt and caraway seeds.
4. Add the foaming yeast to the liquid mixture.
5. Stir in the hard wheat flour and stir vigorously for 1 to 2 minutes.

6. Stir in the whole rye flour. The dough will be very stiff.
7. Scrape down the sides of the bowl. Cover and let rest 30 minutes.
8. Turn out the dough and knead on an oiled or buttered surface for 10 minutes. This should require very little additional flour, if any.
9. Butter the mixing bowl, return the dough to it and let rise until double, about 1 hour.
10. Punch down the dough and let rise 45 minutes more (again doubling in volume).
11. Punch down the dough, let it rest 10 minutes, then cut in half. Shape into two tapered ovals and place on a surface that is generously dusted with cornmeal.
12. Let rise, covered, for 30 minutes or until almost doubled. Preheat the oven to 375°F., preheating the baking stone as well. Slash the tops of the loaves diagonally with a sharp knife or razor, then gently pick up each risen loaf and place on the hot stone. Bake 40 minutes at 375°F. Remove to racks to cool.

Yield: 2 loaves

Yeasted Cornmeal Bread

1 tsp. honey
1/4 c. lukewarm water
1 T. dry active yeast
1 c. milk
1/4 c. butter
3/4 tsp. salt
3 T. honey
2 eggs
1 c. cornmeal
3 3/4 c. whole wheat flour (hard)

1. Dissolve the teaspoon honey in lukewarm water and sprinkle the yeast on top. Let proof for 10 minutes, until foamy.
2. Heat the milk, butter, salt and 3 tablespoons honey until the butter melts.
3. Whisk the cornmeal into the hot milk mixture. Cool to lukewarm, then whisk in the eggs.
4. Add the yeast to the liquid ingredients, then stir in the flour.
5. Follow the directions for the Delayed Kneading Technique for rising and brief kneading.
6. Form two small loaves or sixteen rolls. Allow to rise until almost doubled — 30 to 40 minutes.
7. Brush with beaten egg wash (1 yolk plus 1 tsp. water), then bake the rolls for 15 minutes at 375°F., or small loaves for 35 minutes.

Yield: 2 small loaves or 16 rolls

BUNS and BISCUITS

Buns are basically little rounds of yeast bread, but what makes them special is a slightly higher butter and honey content, making them richer and sweeter. Some buns are intensely spiced, making them an especially savory accompaniment to lunches and suppers.

The category of biscuits covers a number of on-the-spot breads that take their rise from baking soda and/or baking powder. Scones make the best shortcake I know of, and like all biscuit batters, take only minutes to prepare.

Hot Cross Buns

We have these every year for Easter, but there's no reason to wait until April to try them. The dough is slightly harder to handle than most of my yeast doughs, but the buns are exceptionally light.

> 1 T. dry active yeast
> 1/4 c. warm water
> 1 c. hot milk
> 1/4 c. honey
> 3 T. butter
> 1 egg
> 3 1/4 c. whole wheat flour (hard)
> 1/2 tsp. cinnamon
> 1/2 tsp. salt
> 1/2 c. raisins

1. Sprinkle the yeast over the warm water and let proof for 10 minutes.
2. Meanwhile, measure the milk, honey and butter, cut into pieces, into a medium bowl. The milk should be hot enough to melt the butter. Cool to lukewarm.
3. Beat the egg. Add to the foaming yeast, then stir the yeast/egg into the liquid mixture.
4. Stir the cinnamon and salt into the flour, then add the flour to the liquid mixture, stirring vigorously. Stir in the raisins.
5. Cover and let rest 30 minutes.
6. Stir down, cover and let rest another 30 minutes.
7. Repeat #6, for a total of 90 minutes.
8. Turn out and knead the dough briefly, working fast on an oiled or buttered surface. Add no more than 2 T. to 1/4 c. flour to knead.
9. Butter the mixing bowl, return the dough to it, and cover. Let rise 45 minutes.
10. Turn out, cut into 12 pieces. Shape each into a ball and place about an inch apart on a well buttered baking tray. Let rise 30 minutes, then make an X slash on top of each one with a sharp

knife or razor blade. Brush with beaten egg and bake 20 minutes at 375°F. Remove to wire racks to cool.

11. While still warm, but *not* hot, fill in the X slashes with the following glaze: Measure into a small bowl or dish 2 T. non-instant non-fat milk powder. Add enough honey or maple syrup to make a smooth, thick paste that will barely drop from the tip of a spoon.

12. Let the buns cool until the glaze is no longer sticky, but enjoy eating them warm. They re-heat very well when wrapped in foil and placed in a hot oven.

Yield: 12 buns

Spiced Pumpkin Yeast Buns

1 T. dry active yeast
1/4 c. lukewarm water
1/2 c. hot milk
1/4 c. honey
1/4 c. melted butter
1/2 tsp. salt
1/2 tsp. cinnamon
1/4 tsp. nutmeg
pinch powdered cloves
1/2 c. canned pumpkin
1 egg
3 c. whole wheat flour (hard)
1/3 c. raisins
1/4 c. chopped pecans

1. Sprinkle the yeast over the lukewarm water and let proof for 10 minutes.
2. In a medium bowl, combine the hot milk, honey, butter, salt, cinnamon, nutmeg, cloves and pumpkin.
3. Beat the egg and add to the yeast. Stir the yeast/egg mixture into the liquid ingredients.
4. Stir in the hard wheat flour, then the raisins and pecans. The dough will appear to be quite sticky.
5. Let rest and rise at 30 minute intervals for a total of 90 minutes. (See instructions for Basic Sweet Whole Wheat Yeast Dough.)
6. Turn out and knead 3 to 5 minutes. Return to mixing bowl, cover and let rise about 45 more minutes, until doubled.
7. Turn out and cut into 14 pieces. Form each into a round ball and flatten slightly with the palm of your hand as you place them about one inch apart on a buttered cookie tray. This last compression gives them extra spring when baking.
8. Let the rolls rise, covered, about 30 minutes. Brush with beaten egg and bake 18 to 20 minutes at 375°F.

Yield: 14-16 buns

Pumpkin Dinner Rolls

Feather light and golden yellow.

    1 T. dry active yeast
    1/4 c. warm water
    1/2 c. milk
    1/2 tsp. salt
    1/4 c. butter
    2 T. honey
    1/2 c. pumpkin puree
    1/4 tsp. mace
    3 c. whole wheat flour (hard)

1. Sprinkle the yeast over the warm water and let proof for 10 minutes.
2. Heat the milk, salt, butter and honey enough to melt the butter. Cool to lukewarm and stir in the pumpkin and mace.
3. Add the foaming yeast to the cooled milk mixture. Stir in the hard wheat flour.
4. Let rest and rise at 30 minute intervals for 90 minutes total. (See instructions for Basic Sweet Whole Wheat Yeast Dough.)
5. Turn out and knead 3 to 5 minutes. Return to the buttered mixing bowl and let rise until doubled, about 45 minutes.
6. Shape into 12 balls, place them 1 1/2 inches apart on a buttered cookie tray and let rise, covered, for 20 minutes. Brush with melted butter and bake 18 minutes at 375°F.

Yield: 12 buns

Herb Rolls

This well-textured roll dough can easily be turned into onion or rye rolls. (See *Variations*.)

    1 T. honey
    1 c. warm milk
    1 T. dry active yeast
    1/2 tsp. nutmeg
    1 tsp. ground, rubbed sage
    2 tsp. caraway seeds
    3/4 tsp. salt
    1 egg, beaten
    2 T. melted butter
    3 1/2 c. whole wheat flour (hard)

1. Stir the honey into the warm milk until dissolved. Sprinkle the yeast on top and let proof for 10 minutes.
2. When the yeast is foaming, whisk in, in order, the nutmeg, sage, caraway, salt, egg and butter. Stir in the hard wheat flour.
3. Cover and let rise at 30 minute intervals for a total of 90 minutes. (See instructions for Basic Sweet Whole Wheat Yeast Dough.)
4. Turn out and knead 5 minutes. Cover and let rise until almost doubled, about 45 minutes.
5. Punch down, cut into 12 pieces and shape each into a round ball. Place an inch and a half apart on a buttered cookie tray, cover and let rise 25 minutes.
6. Bake 20 minutes at 350°F. Remove to wire racks to cool.

Yield: 12 rolls

VARIATIONS

Onion Rolls

Omit sage, caraway and nutmeg. Saute 1/2 c. chopped onion in the 2 T. butter, cool and add just before the flour.

Rye Rolls

Omit sage and nutmeg. Increase caraway to 1 T. or use 2 tsp. dill seed and 1 tsp. caraway seeds. In place of 3 1/2 c. whole wheat flour, use 2 1/2 c. whole wheat flour and 1 c. whole rye flour.

Potato Buns

An adaptation of a colonial recipe; potato buns were one of Martha Washington's specialties.

1 T. dry active yeast
1/4 c. warm water
1 c. hot riced potatoes
1 tsp. salt
1 c. hot milk
1/4 c. honey
1/2 c. butter
2 eggs
5 1/2 c. whole wheat flour (hard)

1. Sprinkle the yeast over the warm water and let proof for 10 minutes.
2. In a medium bowl, combine the potatoes, salt, milk, honey and butter, cut into pieces. The heat of the potatoes and milk should melt the butter. Cool to lukewarm.
3. Beat the eggs and add to the proofed yeast.
4. Add the yeast mixture to the warmed liquids and stir in the flour.
5. Let rest and rise at 30 minute intervals for a total of 90 minutes. (See instructions for Basic Sweet Whole Wheat Yeast Dough.)
6. Turn out and knead 5 minutes. Return to buttered mixing bowl and cover. Let rise 45 minutes or until doubled.
7. Punch down, cut into 24 pieces and shape into round balls. Place an inch and a half apart on buttered cookie trays.
8. Let rise, covered, for 30 minutes, then bake 16 to 18 minutes at 350°F. Remove to wire racks to cool.

Yield: 24 buns

Dilled Carrot Buns

1 T. dry active yeast
1/2 c. warm water
1/2 c. carrot puree (cooked, blended carrots)
2 T. butter
2 T. honey
3/4 tsp. salt
2 tsp. dill seed
1 tsp. caraway seed
1 egg
3 c. whole wheat flour (hard)
2 T. non-instant non-fat powdered milk

1. Sprinkle yeast over the warm water and let proof for 10 minutes.
2. Warm the carrot puree, butter, honey and salt enough to melt the butter. Cool to lukewarm and add the dill seed and caraway. Whisk in the egg, then add the foaming yeast.
3. Whisk together the flour and milk powder. Stir into the liquid ingredients. You may add several more tablespoons flour to make a dough that just clears the sides of the bowl.
4. Let rest and rise at 30 minute intervals for a total of 90 minutes. (See instructions for Basic Sweet Whole Wheat Yeast Dough.)
5. Turn out and knead 3 to 5 minutes. Return to buttered mixing bowl, cover and let rise 45 minutes until doubled.
6. Turn out, cut into 12 pieces, shape into round balls and place on a buttered cookie tray.
7. Cover and let rise 30 minutes until doubled. Then bake 20 minutes at 350°F.

Yield: 12 buns

A Word on Biscuits

The ideal biscuit conjures up widely different pictures in people's minds. To me, it is high and flaky, achieved by using soft wheat flour and cutting in the butter. To my surprise, I discovered that this isn't everyone's ideal—a friend of mine prefers hers flatter, made with melted butter, Southern style. It's certainly easier to melt the butter and stir in, but if you do, reduce the milk to 1/3 cup. When I specify baking powder, I mean the double-acting kind.

Flaky Whole Wheat Biscuits

A small batch—double for more.

- 1 c. whole wheat pastry flour
- 1/8 tsp. salt
- 1 1/2 tsp. baking powder
- 2 T. butter
- 6 T. milk

1. In a small bowl, combine the flour, salt, and baking powder.
2. With 2 knives, cut in the butter as finely as possible.
3. Add the milk all at once. Stir with a fork until combined. Turn out onto a floured surface and knead briefly. (This produces a more dense crumb and higher rising biscuit, but it's perfectly acceptable just to pat out the dough to a thickness of 3/4 inch.) Roll out to 3/4 inch thick and cut out six 2-inch rounds with a sharp pastry cutter.
4. Place on a buttered cookie sheet and bake 12 minutes at 425°F.

Yield: 6 biscuits

VARIATIONS

Hard Wheat Flour

Use 7/8 c. hard wheat flour in place of pastry wheat.

Wheat Germ Biscuits

Use 3/4 c. soft wheat flour and 1/4 c. wheat germ. Pat out the biscuits instead of kneading.

Herbed Biscuits

Add 1 T. minced parsley and 1/8 tsp. basil to the flour mixture.

Irish Soda Wedges

1 c. whole wheat pastry flour
1/2 tsp. baking powder
1/4 tsp. baking soda
1/8 tsp. salt
2 T. butter
1/4 c. raisins
1/2 tsp. caraway seeds
5-6 T. buttermilk or plain yogurt, stirred
1 tsp. honey
1 tsp. brandy

1. In a small bowl, combine the flour, baking powder, baking soda and salt.
2. Cut in the butter. Add the raisins and caraway seeds. Pour in the buttermilk and stir with a fork until well combined.
3. Turn onto a well-floured surface, knead briefly or pat and fold. Shape into a 1/2 inch thick round and cut into 6 wedges.
4. Place on buttered cookie trays and bake 15 to 18 minutes at 375°F.
5. After 12 to 15 minutes, brush the tops with a mixture of honey and brandy. Return to oven to complete baking, 3-5 minutes. Serve hot.

Yield: 6 wedges

Pumpkin Biscuits

Sweet, golden biscuits — a great change from cornbread. Serve with spicy foods like chili.

2 c. whole wheat pastry flour
1 T. baking powder
1/4 tsp. salt
1/8 tsp. mace
4 T. butter
3/4 c. pumpkin puree
2 T. honey
1 egg

1. In a shallow medium bowl, combine the flour, baking powder, salt and mace.
2. Cut in the butter.
3. Whisk together the pumpkin, honey and egg. Stir into the flour mixture.
4. Turn the dough out onto a well-floured surface. Dust with flour and pat and fold at least once. Cut into 2-inch biscuits and bake on an ungreased cookie tray for 15 minutes at 425°F.
5. Serve warm.

Yield: 14 biscuits

Scones

The basic difference between scones and biscuits is the egg. Since scones, like biscuits, are best eaten fresh and hot, I've scaled down my recipes to suit a table for two, but the recipes double just fine for larger families.

A word on whole wheat pastry flour here: since moisture is critical in scones and biscuits, you may have to add an extra tablespoon of flour per cup if you find the dough too difficult to handle using 1 level cup of pastry flour. As a general rule, I usually add the extra tablespoon when using soft red pastry wheat flour and stay with the level one cup measure when I'm grinding soft white wheat berries.

Honey Drop Scones

With butter and jam for breakfast or for a quick and delicious shortcake, split and butter the hot scones, then top with sweetened fresh fruit and whipped cream.

> 1 c. whole wheat pastry flour
> 1 1/2 tsp. baking powder
> 1/8 tsp. salt
> 2 T. butter
> 1/4 c. milk
> 1/2 large egg, beaten (1 1/2 to 2 T.)
> 1 T. honey

1. Combine the flour, baking powder and salt in a small bowl. Cut in the butter with two knives or a pastry cutter.
2. With a fork, emulsify the milk, honey and egg.
3. Stir the liquids into the dry ingredients with a fork.
4. Drop the batter by the rounded soupspoon onto a buttered cookie tray and bake 12 minutes at 400°F.

NOTE: The scone batter also makes a wonderful cobbler topping for cooked fruits (apples, peaches, cherries, pears). Melt the butter instead of cutting it in and use the whole beaten egg. Spread the batter on top of the hot cooked, thickened fruit in an 8 x 8 inch baking and bake 25 minutes at 400°F.

Yield: 6 scones or 1 cobbler topping

Cheese Scones

Savory scones to serve with soup or spicy omelettes.

    1 c. (plus 1 T.) whole wheat pastry flour
    1 1/4 tsp. baking powder
    1/8 tsp. salt
    dash cayenne
    1 T. butter
    1 rounded half cup shredded sharp cheddar
    1 large egg, beaten
    1/3 c. milk

1. Combine the flour, baking powder, salt and cayenne.
2. Cut in the butter, then stir in the cheese.
3. Combine half the beaten egg (about 1 1/2 to 2 T.) and milk, then stir this mixture into the dry ingredients with a fork.
4. Turn the dough out onto a well floured surface and knead briefly (or simply pat out) and cut into 2 inch rounds.
5. Place the rounds on a buttered baking tray and brush with a glaze made by combining the remaining half egg, beaten with 1/2 teaspoon cold water.
6. Bake 15 minutes at 400°F.

Yield: 6 scones

MUFFINS and QUICK BREADS

Muffins, honey sweet and hot from the oven, are always a treat. They are one of the most versatile batters: fruits, spices and nuts are all welcome additions.

Muffins are a solution for wheat-allergic or milk-allergic people. The entire range of flours — oat, barley, rice, corn, triticale, rye and buckwheat — can be substituted whole or in part for the wheat flour in the basic recipe. Milk solids may be omitted and fruit juice substituted for the water. Even eggs are unnecessary. Eggless muffins have a good rise and produce a cake-like product with a pleasing texture. To prove that nothing is sacred to the muffin, you can leave out the baking powder/baking soda and use yeast for the leavening.

Serve the muffins hot out of the oven. After the muffins have cooled, leftover muffins can be frozen either in aluminum foil (shiny side in) or in airtight plastic bags. If you use aluminum foil, you can save one step and reheat them, still enclosed in the foil, in the oven. If you use plastic bags, remove the muffins from the bags, place in aluminum foil and heat in a 350°F oven for 20 minutes. Should you find yourself with week old muffins, turn them into bread pudding.

High oven heat is essential for proper texture. A muffin should be uniformly crowned (not wobbly peaked or flat). Unless the oven is at 400°F when the muffin goes in, no number of good intentions or well-stirred batters will produce the right muffin. When properly mixed and baked, the muffin will be spongy and light and will break without crumbling. It will also appear to be tunnelled with air pockets. Muffins made without eggs will not be so tunnelled; they will have the appearance of cake.

Fruit breads incorporate all the minerals of fruits, especially potassium and magnesium, with the high protein of hard wheat flour. Prepared with yogurt, the milk protein has been "predigested" by the yogurt culture organisms, making for easier assimilation. The following recipes all incorporate one egg more in the batter than most quick breads for extra protein. To add special interest to these breads, serve them with a variety of nut butters — toasted almond and cashew as well as peanut — to complement grain proteins.

Fruit breads can be baked in any size can. I use three 2 3/4 c. cans for each recipe, filling them just slightly more than half full before baking. Should you use a different size can, increase the number of cans if they are smaller or use two larger cans. Again, only fill between 1/2 and 2/3 full, since the batter rises quite high in baking. Adjust baking times according to the size and number of the cans, reducing time for smaller cans and adding 5 to 10 minutes for larger cans.

Basic Graham Muffins

2 c. whole wheat flour (hard)
1/4 tsp. salt
1 tsp. double acting baking powder
1/2 tsp. baking soda
2 eggs
1/4 c. honey
1 c. water
1/3 c. powdered instant non-fat milk
1/4 c. melted butter

1. Preheat oven to 400°F.
2. Measure into a medium bowl and combine the flour, salt, baking powder and baking soda.
3. In a small bowl, whisk together the eggs, honey, water, milk powder and butter.
4. Pour the liquid ingredients into the dry all at once. Then stir quickly, making sure to moisten all dry ingredients.
5. Hard wheat makes a stiffer batter than pastry wheat. Using a large serving spoon, measure 2 spoonsful of the batter into each muffin cup. As a general rule, the muffin tins should be between half and 2/3 full.
6. Bake the muffins in a 400°F. oven for 20 minutes. If the oven is working properly, there is no need to peek, since opening the oven door only means the muffins may collapse. Allow the muffins to cool 5 minutes after baking. Then remove them from the pans and transfer to a plate or dish, setting the muffins on their sides instead of bottoms to prevent them from getting soggy. Serve with butter, fruit purees or nut butter spreads.

Yield: 12 muffins

Basic Pastry Muffins

More like cake than muffins. This recipe is an excellent way to introduce your family to whole wheat.

> 2 c. whole wheat pastry flour
> 1/4 tsp. salt
> 1 tsp. double acting baking powder
> 1/2 tsp. baking soda
> 2 eggs
> 1/4 c. honey
> 3/4 c. water
> 1/3 c. powdered instant non-fat milk
> 1/4 c. melted butter

1. Preheat oven to 400°F.
2. Measure into a medium bowl and combine the flour, salt, baking powder and baking soda.
3. Measure into a small bowl the eggs, honey, water, milk powder and melted butter. Whisk together until smooth.
4. Pour the liquid ingredients into the dry all at once. Combine quickly, making sure that all dry ingredients on the bottom of the bowl are moistened.
5. Pour the batter into a buttered muffin tin with 12 cups, filling each one slightly more than half full.
6. Place the muffin tin in the center of the oven and bake for 20 minutes at 400°F. without opening the door.
7. Remove from the oven and let cool for 5 minutes. Place the blade of a dinner knife straight down the side of each muffin to pry it loose from the tin. If it does not pop out right away, run the knife around the entire muffin and gently lever it out. Place the muffins on their sides on the plate. This allows the air to circulate and prevents moisture (from escaping steam) to build up on the bottoms of the muffins. Cover with a tea towel.
8. Serve warm with butter, fruit purees or nut butter spreads.

Yield: 12 muffins

VARIATIONS

Wheat Germ Muffins

You can make Wheat Germ Muffins out of either of the two muffin recipes by substituting 1/4 c. raw wheat germ for an equal quantity of wheat flour. Proceed according to instructions.

Wheatless Muffins

Flours from grains other than wheat make delicious muffins. You may use other flours in Basic Pastry Muffins. The following descriptions will serve as a guide to get you started. Combine different flours in any proportion you desire. The fun of making muffins is really in the mixing of flours, and you can come up with your own hybrid muffin by combining different flours to total 2 cups. Flour combinations also boost the nutritional power of the muffins, since complementary proteins are made available to the body at the same time.

100% Barley Muffins

Substitute finely ground barley flour for the wheat flour in Basic Pastry Muffins. These are mild flavored and take well to spices and chopped apples. Try adding 1 tsp. cinnamon and 1/2 c. (or more) chopped apples to the batter or a combination of apples and dates.

100% Buckwheat Muffins

If you are grinding your own flour, be sure to grind it to a fine powder. Substitute buckwheat flour for wheat flour in Basic Pastry Muffins. Buckwheat produces a fine grained, distinctively flavored muffin with an affinity for spiced apple butter or other cinnamon-rich fruit purees.

100% Corn Muffins

For those who enjoy the pure flavor of corn, grind yellow or white field corn to a fine flour and use in place of wheat flour in the Basic Pastry Muffin. This fragrant muffin proves that corn does not always require wheat to make a perfect muffin.

100% Oat Muffins

Grind whole oat groats or rolled oats in a blender to a fine powder and use in place of wheat in Basic Pastry Muffins. The muffins are delicate and fine grained, like sponge cakes. Their natural sweetness combines well with coconut. Try dusting buttered muffin tins with dried shredded coconut before pouring in the muffin batter.

100% Rice Muffins

Texture will depend on whether you've ground your own rice flour or bought the more powdery commercial flour. In either case, rice makes a sweet muffin, and home ground flour tends to bake into a moist, chewy, dessert-like cake. Substitute rice flour for pastry wheat in Basic Pastry Muffins.

Blueberry Muffins

Prepare the batter for Basic Pastry Muffins, increasing the honey to 1/3 cup. Fold in 1 cup fresh or frozen blueberries just before baking.

Fruit Juice Muffins

Fruit juice can be substituted for water and milk solids in any Basic Muffin recipe. When using naturally sweet juices, such as apple, orange or pineapple, reduce the honey to 2 T. For Pastry Muffins, use 3/4 c. fruit juice, for Graham Muffins, use 1 c. fruit juice.

If milk allergy is not a problem, powdered milk can be added along with the fruit juice to boost the protein. One-third cup instant milk powder adds 10 grams of protein and mellows the flavor of the fruit.

Date and Nut Muffins

Follow the recipe for Basic Pastry Muffins, adding 1/2 tsp. cinnamon to the flour. Stir into the batter 1/2 c. chopped pitted dates and 1/2 c. chopped walnuts. Bake as for Basic Pastry Muffins.

Spiced Muffins

This is a lightly spiced muffin. Follow the directions for Basic Pastry Muffins. Add to the flour: 1 tsp. cinnamon, 1/4 tsp. allspice, and a dash nutmeg. Stir into the batter before baking: 1/2 c. raisins and 1/2 c. chopped nuts. Proceed according to directions.

Cinnamon Apple Muffins

2 c. whole wheat pastry flour
1/4 tsp. salt
1 1/2 tsp. baking powder
1/2 tsp baking soda
1 tsp. cinnamon
2 T. honey
1/4 c. melted butter
3/4 c. unsweetened apple juice
2 eggs
(1/2 c. chopped fresh or dried apple)
1/2 c. chopped walnuts

Mix and bake as for Basic Pastry Muffins.

Yield: 12 muffins

Crumb Cake Muffins

Crumb toppings turn regular breakfast muffins into holiday fare. Make up the recipe for Basic Pastry Muffins, pour into buttered muffin cups, then sprinkle the following crumb topping over the batter in each cup. The crumbs will appear to be sinking, but will rise to the top and brown perfectly, provided the oven has been preheated and you bake the muffins immediately.

Crumb Topping

1/2 c. rolled oats
1/3 c. hard wheat flour
3 T. dried shredded coconut
2 T. butter
2 T. honey

1. In a small bowl, measure the oats, flour and coconut.
2. Melt the butter with the honey and pour over the dry ingredients. Mix with a fork until all the dry ingredients are uniformly coated and the mixture forms small crumbs.
3. Sprinkle on top of each muffin before baking.

Eggless Muffins

Make sure to grind the grain to a fine flour and proceed with any muffin recipe with the following change: increase the water by 1/3 cup for hard wheat and 1/4 cup for soft wheat. Without eggs, the flavor of the grain is more pronounced.

Maple Pecan Muffins

2 c. whole wheat pastry flour
1/4 tsp. salt
1 1/2 tsp. double acting baking powder
1/4 c. maple syrup
2 eggs
1/4 c. melted butter
3/4 c. water
1/3 c. powdered instant non-fat milk
1/2 tsp. vanilla
1/2 c. chopped raw pecans

1. Into a medium bowl measure and combine the flour, salt and baking powder.
2. In a small bowl, whisk until smooth the maple syrup, eggs, butter, water, milk and vanilla.
3. Pour the liquid ingredients into the dry and stir quickly. Stir in the pecans.
4. Pour or spoon into buttered muffin tins.
5. Bake 20 minutes at 400 °F.

Yield: 12 muffins

Peanut Butter Muffins

These rise high, filling the kitchen with the aroma of fresh roasted peanuts.

 2 c. whole wheat pastry flour
 1 tsp. double acting baking powder
 1/2 tsp. baking soda
 1/4 tsp. salt
 2 eggs
 1/4 c. honey
 1/2 c. creamy natural peanut butter
 2 T. melted butter
 3/4 c. water
 1/3 c. powdered instant non-fat milk
 1/2 c. chopped roasted peanuts

1. Preheat oven to 400°F.
2. In a medium bowl combine the flour, baking powder, baking soda and salt.
3. In a small bowl, whisk together the eggs, honey, peanut butter, melted butter, water and milk powder.
4. Pour the liquid ingredients into the dry and stir quickly, until just combined. Add the chopped peanuts.
5. Spoon into buttered muffin cups and bake 20 minutes at 400°F.

Yield: 12 muffins

NOTE: Try to use a soft, oily peanut butter. Deaf Smith or Adam are both good choices.

Corn Muffins

100% corn muffins are delicious in their own right, but they do not provide the protein quality or quantity of this recipe. Use this batter for cornbread as well, baking it in a buttered 8 x 8 inch or 9 x 9 inch pan.

1 3/4 c. fine cornmeal (ground almost to a flour)
1/4 c. whole wheat pastry flour
1/4 tsp. salt
1 tsp. baking powder
1/2 tsp. baking soda
1/4 c. honey
2 eggs
3/4 c. water
1/3 c. powdered instant non-fat milk
1/4 c. melted butter

1. Preheat oven to 400°F.
2. Into a medium bowl, measure and combine the corn and wheat flours, salt, baking powder and baking soda.
3. In a small bowl, whisk together the honey, eggs, water, milk powder and melted butter.
4. Pour the liquid ingredients into the dry and stir briskly.
5. Spoon or pour the batter into buttered muffin cups and bake 20 minutes at 400°F.

Yield: 12 muffins or 1 square cornbread

Rice Bread / Muffins

I sometimes make this quick bread instead of cornbread with soups or chili. When made with home ground, brown rice flour, it has a texture very similar to cornbread.

    1 c. brown rice flour
    1 c. whole wheat pastry flour
    1/4 tsp. salt
    1 tsp. baking powder
    1/2 tsp. baking soda
    2 T. honey
    2 eggs
    7/8 c. water
    1/4 c. melted butter
    1/3 c. powdered instant non-fat milk

Mix and bake as for Basic Pastry Muffins.

Yield: 12 muffins

Yogurt Wheat Germ Muffins

Yogurt makes a more tender crumb in these muffins, and it really does make a difference when you use *golden* raisins.

 1 1/2 c. whole wheat pastry flour
 1/2 c. raw wheat germ
 1/4 tsp. salt
 1 tsp. baking soda
 2 eggs
 1/3 c. honey
 1 c. plain yogurt
 1/4 c. melted butter
 1/2 c. golden raisins

1. Into a medium bowl, measure and combine the flour, wheat germ, salt, and baking soda.
2. Into a small bowl, whisk together until smooth the eggs, honey, yogurt and melted butter.
3. Pour the liquid ingredients into the dry. Stir in the raisins.
4. Bake as for Basic Muffins.

Yield: 12 muffins

Oat Flake Muffins

The milk is double rich in this recipe, to boost the protein of each muffin to 5 grams.

    1 c. water
    2/3 c. powdered instant non-fat milk
    1 c. rolled oats
    1 c. whole wheat pastry flour
    1/4 tsp. salt
    1 tsp. baking powder
    1/2 tsp. baking soda
    2 eggs
    1/4 c. honey
    2 T. melted butter

1. Combine the water and milk and pour over the rolled oats. Let soak for 15 minutes or until softened.
2. Preheat the oven to 400°F.
3. Measure into a medium bowl and combine the flour, salt, baking powder and baking soda.
4. In a small bowl, whisk together the eggs, honey and melted butter.
5. Add the soaked oats and milk to the liquid ingredients.
6. Pour the mixture into the dry ingredients and mix and bake as for Basic Pastry Muffins.

Yield: 12 muffins

68   Muffins and Quick Breads

Bran Muffins

Each muffin supplies 1 tablespoon of vital bran fiber.

1 1/4 c. hard wheat flour
3/4 c. miller's bran
1 tsp. baking soda
1/4 tsp. salt
2 eggs
2 T. honey
1/3 c. less 2 T. molasses
1 c. plain yogurt
1/4 c. melted butter
1/2 c. raisins

1. Preheat oven to 400°F.
2. Into a medium bowl, measure and combine the flour, bran, baking soda, and salt.
3. Spoon 2 T. honey into a one-cup measure and fill to 1/3 c. level with molasses.
4. In a small bowl, whisk together until smooth the eggs, honey, molasses, yogurt and melted butter.
5. Pour the liquid ingredients into the dry and stir briskly.
6. Add the raisins.
7. Bake as for Basic Muffins.

Yield: 12 muffins

Spiced Rye Muffins

Spicing is more pronounced in these deliciously scented muffins, since it is designed to complement 100% rye flour. However, the combination of spices works well with graham or triticale flour too.

2 c. whole rye flour
1/4 tsp. salt
1 tsp. baking powder
1/2 tsp. baking soda
1/2 tsp. cinnamon
1/4 tsp. cloves
1/4 tsp. allspice
1/8 tsp. cardamon
1 tsp. orange zest
2 eggs
1/4 c. honey
3/4 c. water
1/3 c. powdered instant non-fat milk
1/4 c. melted butter
1/2 c. raisins

1. In a medium bowl combine the flour, salt, baking powder, baking soda, spices and orange zest.
2. In a small bowl, whisk together the eggs, honey, water, milk powder, and melted butter.
3. Combine the liquid and dry ingredients, then stir in the raisins.
4. Bake as for Basic Muffins.

Yield: 12 muffins

Gingerbread Muffins

2 c. whole wheat pastry flour
1/4 tsp. salt
1 tsp. baking powder
1/2 tsp. baking soda
1 tsp. cinnamon
1 tsp. ginger
2 eggs
2 T. honey
1/4 c. molasses
3/4 c. water
1/3 c. powdered instant non-fat milk
1/4 c. melted butter
1/2 c. raisins

1. In a medium bowl combine the flour, salt, baking powder, baking soda, cinnamon, and ginger.
2. In a small bowl, whisk together the eggs, honey, molasses, water, milk powder and melted butter.
3. Quickly combine the liquid and dry ingredients. Stir in the raisins.
4. Bake as for Basic Muffins.

Yield: 12 muffins

Muffins and Quick Breads 71

Carob Muffins

Serve these with butter and honey. For a quick tea-time or coffe cake, bake the batter in an oblong pan (7 x 11) and serve hot with honey. Or cool and frost with Vanilla Cream Cheese Frosting and top with chopped nuts.

1 1/2 c. whole wheat pastry flour
1/2 c. carob flour
1 tsp. cinnamon
1/4 tsp. salt
1 tsp. double acting baking powder
1/2 tsp. baking soda
1/4 c. honey
2 eggs
3/4 c. water
1/3 c. powdered instant non-fat milk
1/4 c. melted butter

1. Preheat oven to 400°F.
2. In a medium bowl, measure and combine the pastry flour, carob, cinnamon, salt, baking powder and baking soda.
3. In a small bowl, whisk until smooth the honey, eggs, water, milk powder and melted butter.
4. Pour the liquid ingredients into the dry and stir briskly.
5. Bake as for Basic Muffins.

Yield: 12 muffins

Yeast Muffins

This is the solution for those who would prefer not to use baking powder or baking soda for leavening yet still want a rise. A yeast muffin is somewhere between a muffin and a bread, and makes a nice change of pace. It is lighter and less sweet than a Basic Muffin and goes well with butter, honey and honeyed fruit purees. The wheat flour is necessarily dominant, since at least 2/3 of the flour component must be hard wheat flour in order to supply the yeast gases with enough gluten to expand the dough.

> 1 c. lukewarm water
> 1/3 c. powdered instant non-fat milk
> 2 T. honey
> 2 T. melted butter
> 1 T. dry active yeast
> 2 eggs, beaten
> 1/4 tsp. salt
> 2 c. wheat flour (hard)

1. Combine in a medium bowl the water, milk, honey, and butter. Sprinkle the yeast on top and let proof for 10 minutes.
2. Add, stirring vigorously, the eggs and salt, then the flour.
3. Cover and let rise until doubled, about 1 hour.
4. Stir down the batter, then spoon it into buttered muffin pans.
5. Let the muffins rise until doubled (they will crest their individual cups). This will take about 25 to 30 minutes.
6. Bake 25 minutes in a 375°F. oven. Remove the muffins from the tin immediately and let cool on a wire rack. If the muffins stick to the pans, run a blunt knife around the muffins and lever them out.

Yield: 12 muffins

Banana Bread

A light bread, rich in the potassium and magnesium of bananas. Bake in cans (see introduction to quick breads) or small loaf pans.

> 1 3/4 c. wheat flour (hard)
> 1/4 tsp. salt
> 1 tsp. baking soda
> 2/3 c. honey
> 1/3 c. melted butter
> 2 eggs
> 1 tsp. vanilla
> 1 c. mashed banana
> 1/4 c. plain yogurt
> 1/2 c. chopped walnuts

1. Into a medium bowl measure the flour, salt, and baking soda.
2. In another bowl, whisk together the honey, melted butter, eggs, vanilla, banana and yogurt.
3. Add the flour to the liquid ingredients in three parts.
4. Stir in the chopped walnuts.
5. Pour the batter into 3 well-buttered 2 3/4 c. cans or two well-buttered small loaf pans and bake 45 minutes at 350°F. Test with a toothpick to see if they are done.

Yield: 2-3 loaves

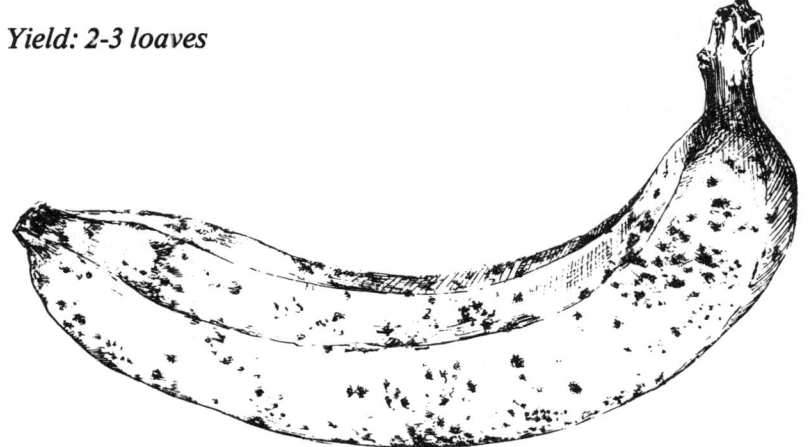

Orange Bread

Fragrant and lightly sweet, this bread slices clean.

    1 1/2 c. wheat flour (hard)
    1/2 c. pastry wheat flour
    1 tsp. baking soda
    1/4 tsp. salt
    1 1/2 tsp. cinnamon
    1/4 tsp. ginger
    1/2 c. plain yogurt
    1/2 c. orange juice
    1 1/2 tsp. freshly grated orange rind
    1/2 c. honey
    2 eggs
    1/4 c. melted butter
    1 tsp. vanilla
    1/2 c. chopped raw pecans

1. Into a medium bowl, measure and combine the flours, baking soda, salt, cinnamon and ginger.
2. In a small bowl, whisk together the yogurt, orange juice, orange rind, honey, eggs, butter and vanilla.
3. Quickly whisk the liquid ingredients into the dry, then stir in the pecans.
4. Pour the batter into three well-buttered cans or two small loaf pans and bake 45 minutes at 350°F.

Yield: 2-3 loaves

Pumpkin Bread

Not a true fruit bread, but so rich in potassium and vitamin A that it rivals all the others in nutrition.

1 3/4 c. whole wheat flour (hard)
1/4 tsp. salt
1 tsp. baking soda
2 tsp. pumpkin pie spice (or 1 tsp. cinnamon, 1/2 tsp. ginger, and 1/4 tsp. cloves)
2/3 c. honey
1/3 c. melted butter
1 c. pumpkin puree
2 eggs
1/4 c. plain yogurt
1/2 c. chopped raw pecans

1. Into a medium bowl measure and combine the flour, salt, baking soda and spice.
2. In another bowl, whisk together the honey, butter, pumpkin, eggs and yogurt.
3. Pour the liquid ingredients into the dry and combine quickly. Stir in the pecans.
4. Pour the batter into 3 well-buttered cans (see introduction to Quick Breads) or small loaf pans and bake 40 to 45 minutes at 350°F.

Yield: 2-3 loaves

Boston Brown Bread

A moist steamed bread that seems to taste even better at the last slice. A natural for cream cheese.

    1 c. rye flour
    1 c. cornmeal
    1 c. wheat flour (hard)
    1/2 tsp. salt
    1 tsp. baking soda
    2 T. buttermilk
    3/4 c. molasses
    2 c. minus 2 T. buttermilk
    1 c. rasins

1. In a medium bowl, combine the rye flour, cornmeal and whole wheat flour and salt.
2. Coat the raisins with part of the flour.
3. Put the baking soda in a small cup and stir in 2 T. of the buttermilk to dissolve the baking soda.
4. In a small bowl, whisk together the molasses, buttermilk, and dissolved soda.
5. Pour the liquid ingredients into the dry, fold in the raisins and pour into 3 buttered cans (about #2 size), cover with foil (buttered on the inside) and steam for 3 hours. Tape the foil to the cans so that they are secure. To steam, simply place the cans on a rack in a covered pot filled with boiling water that reaches half-way up on the cans. Keep the water at a slow boil.
6. Cool before removing from the cans.

Yield: 3 loaves

CRACKERS and FLAT BREADS

Since the whole grain cracker industry is relatively young, there are not many varieties to choose from in the stores and the flavor is not always the best. Remember, a commercial cracker, even a whole grain variety, is up against the same obstacles that plague most other manufactured health foods. The flour isn't as fresh as home ground flour, and the time involved in packaging, transporting and distributing dissipates the vitality of the crackers.

The good news is that you can make your own crackers in quantity, quickly and inexpensively. Their flavor will be a genuine surprise if you haven't ever tried freshly baked whole grain crackers before. Some of the most stubborn white flour fans have been won over on the strength of Whole Wheat Sesame Thins *alone. Nothing on the market, refined or unrefined, can match the crackers you can make at home.*

Most attempts at crackers fail because of irregular thickness of the dough. This is the direct result of rolling technique or the dough recipe or both.

Making crackers is much like baking bread; once you have learned the basic technique and what to expect of your ingredients, you can go on to vary the proportions and introduce new flours.

Wheat makes the most workable dough. Even brief kneading makes the dough highly elastic, and it can be rolled extremely thin and still hold together well. Hard wheats are ideal for crackers because of the elasticity of the doughs made from their flours, but the flavor of hard wheat also tends to dominate the crackers made with it. For those recipes requiring a lighter base so that the taste of the spices—chili or cheese—comes out, all or part soft wheat should be used. When adjusting recipes or creating new ones, bear in mind that hard wheat absorbs more water than soft wheat. Reduce the water by 1 T. for each cup of soft wheat used in addition to the 1 cup called for in Whole Wheat Sesame Thins.

Whole Wheat Sesame Thins

Try these crackers once and you'll never be able to go back to store made crisps. The flavor of freshly ground wheat is an experience all its own, and when that wheat is combined with sesame seeds, the result is unbeatable.

Many of my friends have started their families on whole wheat by serving these crackers. They are deliciously crisp and complement any cheese or spread. They also keep well, so make a big batch.

> 2 c. wheat flour (hard)
> 1 c. soft wheat pastry flour
> 3 T. unhulled sesame seeds
> 1/2 tsp. salt
> 1 c. less 1 T. water
> 1/4 c. melted butter

1. Into a medium bowl, measure and combine the hard wheat flour, soft wheat flour, sesame seeds and salt.
2. In a two cup measure or small bowl measure and emulsify with a fork the water and melted butter.
3. Stir the liquid ingredients into the dry with a fork until well combined. The dough may appear slightly sticky. Allow to rest 10 to 20 minutes for the whole wheat to absorb moisture. Gather into a ball and knead lightly for 2 to 3 minutes.
4. See the next two pages for rolling instructions.
5. Bake the crackers on ungreased cookie sheets in a 350°F. oven for 20 to 25 minutes, until golden and crisp. Cool and store in a tightly lidded container.

Yield: 100-110 small crackers

Rolling with a Pasta Machine

The easiest way to make thin, uniform crackers is to form the dough into small balls and run them through the flat rollers of a pasta machine. If you do not own a pasta machine, manual or electric, it is well worth the price for use in making crackers, let alone pasta. All the wheat cracker recipes in this book roll easily through the pasta machine.

Slice the dough ball in half. Put one half back in the bowl and cover. Slice the other half, as for bread, into 1/2 inch slices. Cut these slabs crosswise at 1/2 inch intervals to produce rods of dough. Now cut these rectangular rods into squares, so that you have 1/2 inch cubes. Roll the cubes into spheres and roll them through the pasta machine on whatever setting you prefer, the thinner the better. You may have to press each ball between the rollers to get it going, but the cracker will roll out uniformly and easily after the initial pressure. Should the crackers crumble, the dough is too dry. If it sticks to the rollers, you have either added too much water or measured too little flour. This is an extremely easy dough to work with. You probably will not need to make adjustments for the flour, but if you do, these adjustments will be minor.

For hand rolling, see next page.

Rolling by Hand

Without a pasta machine you can still make fine crackers by several easy, though less uniform, methods. All wheat-based crackers can be rolled with a rolling pin on a smooth surface, such as formica or a Tupperware rolling sheet, and transferred to ungreased cookie sheets. By that, I do not mean that you should roll out *each* cracker. Rather, roll out large sheets or rounds of dough, transfer these to cookie sheets and then cut into shapes—triangles, squares, rectangles and other polygons. Make what I call "Super Chips." Giant round crackers 3 inches or more in diameter and about 6 to the cookie tray. For each one, start out with a ball about the size of a rounded tablespoon and roll it as you would for pie dough. In rolling these or any other crackers, use oil or melted butter to keep the crackers from sticking to the rolling surface, not flour. Extra flour at this time will only make the crackers tough. Lower the heat for Super Chips, so that they bake through to the center without burning the edges.

No matter which of the above methods you use, always roll the crackers as thin as you can manage. As confidence grows and you master the technique, they will roll thinner and thinner. Of course, if you have the pasta machine you will get them perfect the first time.

VARIATIONS

Mixed Grain Thins

Hard wheat tends to dominate other flavors, and unless you are intent on making very hearty crackers, always combine it with some soft wheat. The soft wheat also makes the dough lighter and easier to roll.

In order to vary the basic recipe and to incorporate other flavors, use the following proportions:

- 1 c. hard wheat flour
- 1 c. soft wheat flour
- 1 c. whole grain flour of your choice (oat, rice, buckwheat, barley, triticale, fine corn meal)

Whole Wheat Sesame Thins with Milk

For increased and complementary protein, substitute fluid milk for water in the Whole Wheat Sesame Thin recipe or any of its variations. Whole or skim milk works equally well.

Cheese Crisps

Try to find as sharp a cheddar as possible for these crackers and roll them as thin as possible. They are good enough to eat for snacks all by themselves, with wheat and cheese proteins providing a complementary protein treat. Soft wheat allows the flavor of the cheese to emerge.

>   3 c. whole wheat pastry flour
>   1/2 tsp. salt
>   1 1/2 c. shredded sharp cheddar
>   1 c. less 3 T. water
>   1/4 c. melted butter

1. In a medium bowl combine the flour, salt and cheese.
2. In a small bowl emulsify the water and butter with a fork.
3. Stir the liquids into the dry ingredients with a fork until thoroughly combined. Let the dough rest 15 minutes. Gather into a ball, knead lightly (1 to 2 minutes), then proceed as for Whole Wheat Sesame Thins.
4. For Chili Cheese Crisps, add 1 T. chili powder to the dry ingredients. These make excellent crackers with Longhorn cheese on top or as a side dish with fruit.

Yield: 100-110 small crackers

Rye Crackers

The taste most of us remember as rye actually comes from the caraway seeds in the dough. In these crackers, the seeds are ground with the rye flour to distribute their flavor evenly throughout the dough. Since rye is very low in gluten, which forms cohesive bands in the dough, wheat flour is mixed with the rye to produce a more elastic dough.

> 2 c. wheat flour (hard)
> 1 c. rye flour
> 1/2 tsp. salt
> 2 to 3 tsp. caraway seeds ground with the rye flour or separately in a seed grinder
> 1 c. less 1 T. water
> 1/4 c. melted butter

1. Combine the wheat flour, rye flour, salt, and caraway seeds in a medium bowl.
2. Emulsify the water and melted butter.
3. Combine liquid and dry ingredients with a fork.
4. Proceed as for Whole Wheat Sesame Thins.

Yield: 100-110 small crackers

Yeast Crackers

Simply roll your favorite bread or roll dough through the pasta machine (as thin as you can manage it) or in thin sheets on a buttered surface and let rise on lightly buttered cookie sheets until double. Bake at 350°F. for 10 to 15 minutes for a matzoh-like treat.

Be sure to prick these crackers with a fork before baking so that air can escape and the crackers bake thoroughly dry.

Soda Crackers

If I called them baking powder crackers, which they really are, you would never try them. Then you would miss out on the best of the lot. Crisp, crunchy, flaky—everything you could ask for in a soda cracker and more.

Actually, since double acting baking powders are in part baking soda, it is only stretching the truth slightly to call these "Soda Crackers."

Why baking powder? Because soda acts with acids. Years ago soda crackers were made with sour milk and hence needed a leavening agent that would react with and neutralize the sour ingredient. Since these get rolled in the pasta rollers, we want to save the lift for the oven. Baking powder produces gas twice, once upon contact with moisture, and also when the batter is put in a hot oven.

Be sure to use pastry wheat or soft white wheat.

> **3 c. wheat pastry flour**
> **1/2 tsp. salt**
> **2 tsp. baking powder**
> **1 c. less 3 T. water**
> **1/4 c. melted butter**

1. Into a medium bowl measure the flour, salt and baking powder.
2. In a small bowl emulsify with a fork the water and melted butter.
3. Combine the liquid and dry ingredients well with a fork, then let the dough rest to absorb moisture. Proceed as for Whole Wheat Sesame Thins.

Yield: 100-110 small crackers

Corn Tortillas

An admitted compromise between corn and wheat that works out well on both sides. There's enough whole corn meal to make these fit for enchiladas, while there's enough wheat flour to make them rollable. Commercial tortilla factories use limed corn which is much more adhesive than regular cornmeal. The reason for this is that the bran (and usually the germ) is removed in the liming process. While this makes niacin in the corn more available for absorption, I favor keeping grains whole, hence the following recipe:

1 c. fine corn meal
1/2 tsp. salt
1 c. boiling water
2 T. lard or butter
1 1/2 c. whole wheat pastry flour

1. In a medium bowl, combine the cornmeal and salt.
2. Pour the boiling water over the mixture, stirring quickly with a fork. Cut in the butter or lard and let melt.
3. When the corn mixture has cooled, stir in the whole wheat pastry flour, again combining with a fork.
4. Let rest, covered, for half an hour.
5. Have some melted butter or lard handy to use in rolling.
6. Pull off golf-ball sized pieces of dough. Drop some melted butter or lard onto the rolling surface and roll each ball into a circle approximately 1/16th inch thick. Keep turning the tortilla to keep it greased and uniform.
7. Fry quickly on a hot dry griddle or cast iron skillet on both sides. Stack the tortillas on top of each other as they are cooked to keep soft. Keep covered with a clean towel.
8. Use as you would commercial tortilla shells.

Yield: 12 tortillas

Whole Wheat Tortilla Shells

These soft tortillas can be served warm with butter (as customary in Mexican restaurants) or folded over, filled with cheese and fried on a griddle to melt the cheese and crisp the shell. You may have your own favorite taco, burrito or quesadilla recipes just waiting for these shells.

    2 c. whole wheat pastry flour
    1 c. wheat flour (hard)
    1/2 tsp. salt
    1/4 c. melted butter or lard
    1 c. water

1. In a medium bowl, combine the flours and salt.
2. Emulsify the melted butter or lard and water and stir into the dry ingredients with a fork until well combined.
3. Let the dough sit for 10 to 15 minutes, to give the flour a chance to absorb moisture.
4. Knead 1 to 2 minutes. You should not have to add any more flour.
5. Have some melted butter or lard handy to use in rolling.
6. Pull off dough balls about the size of golf balls and roll out on a greased surface. Keep the rolling pin well greased also. Roll into circles as thin as possible, turning as you roll to keep them from sticking. Fry quickly on a hot dry skillet, turning as soon as the undersides are barely speckled with brown spots. You do *not* want these shells to get crisp.
7. Stack the tortillas on top of one another as they are cooked and cover with a clean towel to keep them soft.
8. Use as you would any commercial tortilla.

Yield: 12 tortillas

FRITTERS, PUFFS and PONE

Fritters are really pancakes plus. Chopped vegetables, cooked grains, fruit slices or nuts are nestled in a batter of eggs, milk and flour, then sauteed in butter. Notice that I said sauteed in contrast to deep-fried as so many fast food fritters are today. When the eggs are separated and the whites are beaten until stiff then folded in, there's no need for any other leavening. If you use whole eggs, however, you'll need to give the batter a lift with baking powder.

Corn Pecan Fritters

1/2 c. whole wheat pastry flour
1/8 tsp. salt
1/8 tsp. nutmeg
2 eggs, separated
1/2 c. milk
1/4 tsp. vanilla
1 c. cooked sweet corn
1/4 c. chopped pecans
2 T. butter, to saute

1. In a medium bowl, combine the flour, salt and nutmeg.
2. In a small bowl, whisk together the egg yolks, milk and vanilla.
3. Whisk the liquid ingredients into the dry.
4. Beat the egg whites until stiff. Fold into the batter, then fold in the corn and pecans.
5. Melt half the butter in a large heavy skillet (large enough to hold 7 fritters at a time) over medium heat and drop in the batter by the heaping tablespoon. Saute until browned underneath, turn and cook until undersides are golden. Repeat with remaining butter and batter. Serve warm with maple syrup.

Yield: 14-16 fritters

Quick Corn Fritters

2 large eggs
1/3 c. whole wheat pastry flour
1/8 tsp. salt
1/8 tsp. nutmeg
1/2 tsp. double acting baking powder
1 c. cooked sweet corn
2 T. butter, for frying

1. In a medium bowl, whisk the eggs until light.
2. In a separate bowl, combine the flour, salt, nutmeg and baking powder, then whisk these ingredients into the beaten eggs.
3. Stir in the corn.
4. Melt half the butter in a large skillet over medium heat. Drop in the batter by the soupspoon and saute until golden, then turn and continue to fry until undersides are browned and the fritters are crowned in the centers. Repeat with remaining butter and batter. Serve hot with maple syrup.

Yield: 14-16 fritters

Herbed Rice Fritters

1/2 c. whole wheat pastry flour
1 T. parsley flakes
1/4 tsp. Italian seasoning
1/8 tsp. salt
1/8 tsp. black pepper
several dashes cayenne
2 eggs, separated
1/4 c. milk
1/4 c. onion broth (reconstituted onion soup)
1 1/4 to 1 1/2 c. cooked brown rice
2 T. butter for frying

1. In a medium bowl, combine the flour, parsley, italian seasoning, salt, pepper, and cayenne.
2. In a small bowl, whisk together the egg yolks, milk and onion broth.
3. Whisk the liquid ingredients into the dry.
4. Stir in the brown rice.
5. Beat the egg whites until stiff, then fold into the batter.
6. Heat half the butter in a large skillet until bubbling. Drop in the batter by the heaping tablespoon and saute until undersides are golden. Turn and continue cooking until browned on both sides. Repeat with the remaining butter and batter. Serve as a main or savory side dish.

Yield: 14-16 fritters

Sweet Corn Pone

Quicker to assemble than Spoon Bread and equally good—Corn Pone is a meal in its own right or can serve as an accompaniment.

> 2 c. milk
> 1 c. yellow cornmeal
> 1/4 tsp. salt
> 3 T. butter
> 2 eggs, beaten
> 1/2 tsp. baking powder

1. Warm the milk. Quickly whisk in the cornmeal and continue whisking over medium heat until the mixture is thick and smooth. Remove from heat.
2. Add the salt. Cut the butter into the thick cornmeal mixture and whisk until melted.
3. Cool the pone slightly, (a few minutes) then whisk in the beaten eggs.
4. Whisk in the baking powder last, then pour into a shallow buttered 1 1/2 quart baking dish.
5. Bake 35 minutes at 350°F. until puffed and golden.
6. Serve warm with additional butter and maple syrup.

Serves 4

─────────────── VARIATION ───────────────

Cheese Pone

Add 1 c. grated sharp cheddar to the cooked cornmeal mixture after adding the eggs. Whisk in the baking powder last, as above, then transfer mixture to a buttered baking dish. Top with 1/4 c. more shredded cheddar and bake 40 minutes at 350°F.

Fritters, Puffs and Pone

Spoon Bread

Spoon bread is more a cross between a custard and a souffle rather than a bread, and as such it's a terrific main dish that never fails to rise spectacularly in the oven. It settles slightly, but not at all as quickly or dramatically as a souffle. An elegant entree any time of day.

4 eggs, separated
2 c. milk
3 T. butter
1 c. yellow cornmeal
1 tsp. baking powder
1/4 tsp. salt

1. Beat the 4 egg yolks until thick and set aside.
2. Beat the whites until stiff and set aside.
3. Heat the milk, whisk in the cornmeal and salt, and stir vigorously over medium heat until the mixture is thick. Add the baking powder and butter and stir until the butter is melted.
4. Remove from the heat and whisk in the egg yolks. Then fold in the stiffly beaten egg whites.
5. Transfer the mixture to a buttered 2 quart baking dish and bake at 375°F. for 35 minutes.
6. Serve hot with butter and maple syrup or sorghum.

Serves 4

Cheddar Spoon Bread

A perfect lunch or light supper for 2 with a tossed salad. Double the recipe for a family.

    1/2 c. yellow corn meal
    1/8 tsp. salt
    1 c. water
    1/4 c. chopped onion
    2 T. butter
    2 eggs, separated
    1/2 c. milk
    1/2 c. shredded sharp cheddar
    dash cayenne

1. In a medium saucepot, combine the cornmeal, salt and water. Set aside.
2. Meanwhile, saute the onion in 1 T. butter until translucent. Remove from heat.
3. Place the cornmeal mixture over medium heat and stir until thick.
4. Stir in the onion and 1 T. butter. Remove from heat.
5. Stir the yolks into the thickened cornmeal, then the milk, cheddar and cayenne.
6. Beat the egg white until stiff, then fold into the batter.
7. Pour the spoon bread into a buttered 1 1/2 quart souffle or baking dish. Bake 45 minutes at 375°F. Serve immediately.

Serves 2

94   Fritters, Puffs and Pone

Puffed Fruit Rolls

Cheese, fruit, whole wheat and eggs combine to make a high protein, high mineral pancake puff.

Make one large pancake (10 to 12 inch skillet) and split for two, or make two 6 inch pancakes and serve individually.

> **3 large eggs**
> **1/3 c. unsweetened pineapple juice**
> **1 tsp. lemon juice**
> **1 T. honey**
> **1/3 c. whole wheat pastry flour**
> **1 1/2 T. butter**
> **1 c. shredded cheddar cheese (sharp)**

1. In a medium bowl, beat the eggs.
2. Add the lemon and pineapple juice and honey, then whisk in the flour.
3. In a 450°F. oven, melt 1 1/2 T. butter in a 10 to 12 inch skillet or 3/4 T. butter in each of two 6 to 8 inch baking pans or skillets.
4. Pour the batter into the hot skillet(s) and bake for 12 minutes, until puffed and golden.
5. Sprinkle the cheese over the cooked pancake(s), return to the oven until the cheese is melted, then roll the pancake(s).
6. Serve topped with a generous portion of Pineapple Sauce (see the following recipe).

Pineapple Sauce

1 (8 oz.) can of chunk, crushed, or tidbit pineapple in its own juice
additional pineapple juice to combine with fluid in can to make 1 cup
1 T. honey
1 tsp. grated orange zest
2 cloves
2 tsp. arrowroot
2 T. water

1. Into a 1 cup measure, drain the pineapple.
2. Add enough additional pineapple juice to equal 1 cup.
3. Transfer the juice to a small saucepan and add the honey, orange zest and cloves. Simmer, covered, for 5 minutes.
4. Dissolve the arrowroot in water.
5. Add the dissolved arrowroot to the pineapple mixture and cook until thickened and clear. Stir in the drained pineapple.
6. Spoon over the pancake puffs.

Serves 2

French Toast

An exotic name for puffed bread; don't wait for leftover bread before making it, though. It's just as good with fresh.

5 thin slices whole wheat bread
3 large eggs
1/2 c. milk
dash cinnamon
butter for frying
maple syrup or jelly

1. In a shallow baking pan that will hold all five slices of bread, whisk together the eggs, milk and cinnamon.
2. Lay the bread slices flat in the pan and let them soak up the egg/milk mixture.
3. Turn the slices occasionally to get them evenly soaked. When there is no more excess liquid, fry the slices in butter in a large skillet or electric frying pan.
4. Serve with more butter and maple syrup or jelly.

Serves 2

GRIDDLE CAKES
Unyeasted and Yeasted

These are the traditional rounded cakes. Every natural foods kitchen has the ingredients necessary to make nutritious pancakes that are a delight to eat. Almost any grain, nut or seed can be turned into a pancake, so don't hesitate to incorporate your favorite flavors in any recipe.

The only constant in making stack cakes is the griddle. It has to be of heavy gauge metal, preferably cast iron but a well-seasoned cast aluminum griddle will work fine. Cast iron transfers important trace iron to the pancakes, yielding a slightly superior product nutritionally. If the griddle is new, season it by heating, then coating it with a thin layer of good quality oil or lard. Allow the griddle to cool. The griddle may also be preheated in an oven, coated with lard, and then allowed to cool down in the oven. When using a griddle for the first time after seasoning, spread a thin layer of lard or cooking oil over the surface after heating and just before pouring or spooning on the batter (See discussion of cooking with oils.) For completely oil free frying, a soapstone griddle is the answer. These never require oil of any kind. They are self-seasoning, absorbing the fats in the batter over a period of time. Their evenly distributed heat produces perfect, golden pancakes with a classic rise. Whichever griddle is used, however, there is a definite method to making well crowned pancakes. Hold the ladle or spoon containing the batter close to the griddle and let the batter flow out from the center of the mound. Dropping the batter from a height of even a few inches will result in an uneven cake.

Notice that the recipes for these pancakes call for non-instant milk powder. For a quickly cooked food, the non-instant powder generally results in better texture and flavor than instant non-fat milk powder. If you cannot get the non-instant, use regular instant milk powder. See the Introduction for a discussion of instant milk versus fresh in cooking.

Wheat Griddlecakes

Hard wheat absorbs more moisture than soft white wheat or soft red pastry wheat. *Generally,* 7/8 cup of hard wheat is the baking equivalent of 1 cup of pastry wheat. In converting favorite refined flour recipes to whole grain versions, bear in mind that the amount of flour must be reduced if hard wheat is used or you must increase the liquids. Pastry wheat can usually be substituted cup for cup of refined flour.

In this recipe I have used the same amount of hard wheat as I do soft wheat in Soft Wheat Cakes, but have increased the water for a light, delectable pancake. When substituting nutritional boosters, such as wheat germ, soy flour or other flours for part of the hard wheat flour, measure the boosters into a one cup measure, then fill to level with hard wheat flour.

This classic cake should first be served with butter and pure maple syrup. Then branch out and try adding a dollop of yogurt to the stack and a ladle of fruit sauce. One half cup of yogurt adds 6 grams of complementary protein.

> 1 c. whole wheat flour (hard)
> 1/4 tsp. salt
> 1 1/2 tsp. double acting baking powder
> 1/3 c. non-instant non-fat milk powder
> 2 large eggs
> 1 c. water
> 2 T. melted butter

1. In a medium bowl, measure and whisk together the flour, salt, baking powder and non-instant milk powder.
2. Into two small bowls, separate the eggs.
3. Add the water to the yolks and whisk this mixture into the dry ingredients, whisking until smooth. Let sit while beating the egg whites until stiff but not dry.
4. Pour a small amount of batter into the beaten whites, folding thoroughly with a rubber spatula. When this mixture is smooth and homogeneous, gradually fold it back into the rest of the batter. Slowly whisk in the butter.

5. Ladle or spoon onto a hot griddle, holding the ladle close to the griddle and spreading out slightly into uniform circles.
6. Bake until the tops bubble and the undersides are brown, about 2 to 3 minutes. The edges should be dry. Turn and griddle for another 1 to 2 minutes.
7. Serve immediately in stacks or a row of overlapping cakes.

Serves 2-3

─────────────── VARIATION ───────────────

Wheat-Rye Griddlecakes

Use 1/2 cup rye and 1/2 cup hard whole wheat flour. Add one tablespoon maple syrup to batter.

Soft Wheat Cakes

If you've never eaten whole wheat pancakes, try this recipe first. The tender crumb and delicate flavor of pastry wheat flour make these rounds of wheat truly "pan cakes."

> **1 c. whole wheat pastry flour**
> **1/4 tsp. salt**
> **1 1/2 tsp. double acting baking powder**
> **1/3 c. non-instant non-fat powdered milk**
> **2 large eggs**
> **7/8 c. water**
> **1 T. melted butter**

1. In a medium bowl, measure and combine the flour, salt, baking powder and non-instant milk powder.
2. Into two small bowls, separate the eggs.
3. Add the water to the yolks and combine this mixture with the dry ingredients, whisking until smooth.
4. Beat the whites until stiff but not dry. Gradually fold in a small amount of batter into the beaten whites, then fold this back into the batter.
5. Slowly whisk in the butter. Bake on a hot griddle until tops are bubbled and the undersides browned. Turn and griddle for 1 to 2 minutes, until golden.

Serves 2-3

VARIATIONS

Oat Cakes

Substitute 1 cup oat flour (blended rolled oats) for the whole wheat pastry flour.

Applejacks

Use 3/4 c. apple juice in place of the water and dry milk.

Rice Cakes

Use 1/2 c. brown rice flour and 1/2 c. whole wheat pastry flour.

Buckwheat Cakes

If you want them to taste like Aunt Jemimah's, use soft wheat pastry flour. Spoon 2 to 3 level T. buckwheat flour into the bottom of a 1 cup measure, fill to level with pastry wheat and proceed as for Soft Pastry Cakes. The result will be light and heavenly. If you love buckwheat, these are the only cakes to make.

Good buckwheat pancakes can also be made from hard wheat flour, again using up to 1/4 cup buckwheat flour and filling to 1 cup level with hard wheat flour. The resulting cakes will be light, but not as delicately flavored as those made with soft pastry wheat.

Blueberry Pancakes

If using fresh berries, fold in 1 cup of fruit as the final addition to the batter before baking. If using frozen berries, ladle the batter onto the hot griddle first, then sprinkle the top of each cake with berries. Since freezing bursts the cell walls, frozen berries will turn the batter blue. By adding the frozen berries to the pancake as it begins to set on the griddle, the cake retains its golden color and the blueberries hold their juice.

> 1 c. whole wheat pastry flour
> 1/4 tsp. salt
> 1 1/2 tsp. double acting baking powder
> 1/3 c. non-instant non-fat milk powder
> 2 eggs
> 7/8 c. water
> 1 T. melted butter
> 1 c. blueberries

Mix and griddle as for Soft Wheat Cakes.

Serves 2-3

Pumpkin Pancakes

Slightly spiced and a very appetizing golden color.

- 1 c. whole wheat pastry flour
- 1 1/2 tsp. double acting baking powder
- 1/4 tsp. salt
- 1/8 tsp. mace
- 1/4 c. non-instant milk powder
- 2 large eggs
- 3/4 c. water
- 1/2 c. pureed pumpkin
- 2 T. melted butter

1. In a medium bowl, measure and combine the flour, baking powder, salt, mace and milk powder.
2. Separate the eggs into two small bowls. Add the water and pumpkin to the yolks. Whisk this mixture into the dry ingredients.
3. Beat the egg whites until stiff but not dry. Slowly fold a small amount of batter into the whites, then fold this mixture back into the batter. Slowly whisk in the butter.
4. Bake on a griddle and enjoy with maple syrup.

Serves 2-3

VARIATION

Carrot Pancakes

Since I always end up planting more carrots than we can ever eat straight as a vegetable, I end up using them as a substitute for pumpkin, which is difficult to grow at the northern latitudes. Simply substitute cooked, pureed carrots for pumpkin in the recipe above for a surprisingly delicious cake. Serve with maple syrup and butter.

Corn Cakes

The lightest corn cakes imaginable. They should be called "zephyr" cakes.

1/2 c. cornmeal (yellow)
7/8 c. boiling water
1 T. honey
1/2 c. whole wheat pastry flour
1/4 tsp. salt
1 1/2 tsp. baking powder
1/3 c. non-instant powdered non-fat milk
2 large eggs, separated
1 T. melted butter

1. Place the cornmeal in a small bowl. Stir the boiling water into it, then the honey. Cover and let stand until it cools to room temperature.
2. Meanwhile, combine in a medium bowl the flour, salt, baking powder and non-instant milk powder.
3. Beat the egg yolks into the cooled cornmeal.
4. Whisk the cooled cornmeal/yolk mixture into the dry ingredients.
5. Beat the egg whites until stiff but not dry. Fold a small amount of the batter into the whites, then fold this back into the batter.
6. Stir in the melted butter.
7. Bake on a hot griddle until tops are bubbled and the undersides browned. Turn and griddle for 1 to 2 minutes, until golden. Serve with maple syrup and/or spiced apples.

Serves 2-3

Whole Wheat Yeast Pancakes

Why yeast pancakes? There are several reasons. Yeast raised pancakes have a different texture from those using baking powder. Yeast pancakes trap the gases formed by growing and multiplying yeasts within the gluten network of the batter. Since wheat has more gluten than any other grain, and hard wheat has more gluten than soft wheat, it is necessary to maintain at least 1/2 cup of hard wheat flour in each batch of yeast pancakes, although if you want to substitute flours the best results are achieved using 3/4 cup hard wheat flour and making quarter cup substitutions of other flours.

Yeast pancakes that have to be started the night before or in the earliest hours of morning somehow never seem to get made. The rule in our house has always been a limit of one hour's preparation for breakfast. If it can't be made in an hour's time, it isn't on the menu. For this reason, the basic yeast recipe is one that will produce light, nutritious pancakes within 60 minutes of measuring the ingredients.

Nutritionally, yeast pancakes differ from baking powder pancakes and crepes. Minerals such as zinc, iron and calcium can be bound up in the intestine by phytic acid, which is present in the bran layer of cereal grains. While the body produces an enzyme, phytase, which can break down the salts formed by phytic acid and minerals, whole wheat and rye also contain this enzyme, but it is only released in the warm moist conditions of dough rising. Yeasted pancakes, then, optimize the nutrients in the whole grains, while adding the extra protein of the yeast itself.

1 c. lukewarm water
1 T. honey
1 T. dry active yeast
1 c. whole wheat flour (hard)
1/4 tsp. salt
1/3 c. non-instant powdered non-fat milk
1 large egg
1 T. melted butter

1. In a medium bowl, measure the water. Stir the honey into the water until dissolved, then sprinkle the yeast on top. Let proof for 10 minutes, until foamy.
2. Meanwhile, combine with a whisk in a separate bowl, the flour, salt, and milk powder.
3. Whisk the egg into the yeast, then whisk in the dry ingredients. Whisk vigorously until well-combined, then whisk in the melted butter.
4. Cover and let rise in a warm spot for 45 to 60 minutes.
5. Stir down the batter and bake on a hot seasoned griddle. Turn when the tops are bubbled and the sides dry and continue cooking until the undersides are browned.

Serves 2-3

---VARIATIONS---

Wheat Germ Yeast Pancakes

These pancakes are nutritionally superior to plain yeasted wheat cakes by the addition of wheat protein.

Into a one cup measure, spoon 3 T. raw wheat germ. Fill to one cup level with hard wheat flour. Proceed as for Whole Wheat Yeast Pancakes, using the wheat germ/flour mixture in place of 1 cup whole wheat flour.

Yeasted Buckwheat Cakes

For buckwheat enthusiasts, a modern version of an early American standby. Traditionally, buckwheat cakes call for baking soda dissolved in water to be added to the batter before baking. This procedure, which is also standard for many sourdough recipes, lightens the pancakes. In this recipe, however, the yeast does it all.

1 c. lukewarm water
1 T. honey
1 T. dry active yeast
1/2 c. whole wheat flour (hard)
1/2 c. buckwheat flour
1/3 c. non-instant powdered non-fat milk
1/4 tsp. salt
1 large egg
1 T. melted butter

Proceed as for Whole Wheat Yeast pancakes, using the combined wheat and buckwheat flours in place of all whole wheat flour.

BLENDER PANCAKES

Blender pancakes are nothing short of magic. A blender eliminates the need for grinding grains into flours and makes pancakes only one step from the whole grain or seed to the batter. No pancake could contain fresher vitamins or minerals than the pancake made from the whole grain with all its nutrients intact right up to the moment of mixing.

Overnight soaking of the grains is recommended to soften the grain enough to make the grinding easier on the blender and to produce a smooth batter. Unsoaked grains can be gritty, because they have not had time to absorb moisture, although occasionally such textures are desirable (in corn pancakes, for example). Since you will be using the soaking water as the liquid component of the batter, do not think of the pre-soaking as an extra chore. Rather, if you measure the grain and water into the blender the night before, pancake preparation will only be a matter of adding the other ingredients and turning on the blender.

The blender makes possible a whole range of grain combinations that produce superbly textured pancakes. Pre-soaking, then rapid blending seems to work up normally crumbly grains into cohesive batters that hold their rise well. Oats and barley are good examples.

Grain flakes can be used in place of whole grains, but be sure to increase their measure. If one-third cup of whole grains are called for, use a scant two-thirds cup of cereal flakes. Since the flaking process means steaming and rolling, flakes do not need to be pre-soaked, but can be added directly to the batter before blending the pancakes.

Blender Wheat Cakes

These are springy like yeast cakes, but with the fragrance of freshly milled wheat. Use either hard or soft wheat berries, according to taste preference. The liquid measure remains the same for either variety.

> 2/3 c. whole wheat berries
> 1 c. water
> 2 large eggs
> 2 T. melted butter
> 1/4 tsp. salt
> 1 T. honey
> 1/2 c. powdered instant non-fat milk
> 1 1/2 tsp. double acting baking powder

1. The night before, soak the wheat berries in water. Do not drain them.
2. In the morning, add the eggs, butter, salt and honey.
3. Process at blend or grind until the batter is smooth. You may have to scrape down the sides of the blender container with a rubber spatula to be sure that all of the wheat berries are ground into the batter.
4. When it is smooth and creamy in appearance, add gradually, while blending, the milk and baking powder.
5. When the milk and baking powder are thoroughly incorporated, turn the blender off and let the batter stand for 20 to 30 minutes before baking the pancakes.
6. Pour the batter from the blender onto a hot seasoned griddle. Bake until the tops are well-bubbled and the sides are dry, about 1 1/2 minutes. Flip and bake until the undersides are well-browned, about 45 seconds to 1 minute more.

Serves 2-3

---VARIATIONS---

Blender Wheat Oat Cakes

Use 1/3 cup hard wheat berries and 1/3 cup oat groats.

Blender Bran Cakes

Surprisingly light pancakes. Fine particles of bran and shreds of wheat have the texture of coconut.

> 1/2 c. hard wheat berries
> 1 c. water
> 1/3 c. miller's bran
> 2 whole eggs
> 2 T. melted butter
> 1/4 tsp. salt
> 1 T. honey
> 1/2 c. powdered instant non-fat milk
> 1 1/2 tsp. double acting baking powder

1. Presoak the wheat berries in water.
2. In the morning add the bran and the rest of the ingredients.
3. Proceed as for Blender Wheat Cakes.

Serves 2-3

Blender Nutty Wheat Cakes

This basic recipe calls for sunflower seeds, but roasted peanuts, raw or roasted cashews, almonds, millet, walnuts, pumpkin seeds, brazils, filberts or pecans make equally delicious pancakes.

Should you be trying to avoid wheat, use oat groats in place of wheat berries, or experiment with barley and rye.

    1/2 c. hard wheat berries
    1 c. water
    1/4 c. raw hulled sunflower seeds
    2 whole eggs
    2 T. melted butter
    1/4 tsp. salt
    1 T. honey
    1/2 c. powdered instant non-fat milk
    1 1/2 tsp. double acting baking powder

1. Pre-soak the wheat berries in water.
2. In the morning, add the sunflower seeds.
3. Proceed as for Blender Wheat Cakes.

Serves 2-3

Blender Corn Cakes

Since dried corn is slow to absorb moisture, it benefits from all the pre-conditioning it can get. White or yellow, corn always smells marvelous when it hits the griddle.

    1/3 c. soft wheat berries
    1/2 c. water
    1/2 c. boiling water
    1/2 c. cornmeal
    2 whole eggs
    2 T. melted butter
    1/4 tsp. salt
    1 T. honey
    1/2 c. powdered instant non-fat milk
    1 1/2 tsp. double acting baking powder

1. Pre-soak the wheat berries.
2. In the morning, mix the cornmeal with boiling water and let stand until cooled to room temperature. Add to the wheat berries in the blender and proceed as for Blender Wheat Cakes.

Serves 2-3

Blender Barley Oat Cakes

Wheat is not essential to light, fluffy pancakes. Rather, some of the sweeter and more cakelike combinations eliminate wheat altogether. Barley and oats produce a golden pancake reminiscent of refined flour, but with the full and satisfying flavor of whole grains.

1/3 c. oat groats
1/3 c. whole hulless barley
1 c. water
2 whole eggs
2 T. melted butter
1/4 tsp. salt
1 T. honey
1/2 c. powdered instant non-fat milk
1 1/2 tsp. double acting baking powder.

1. Pre-soak the oats and barley in water.
2. In the morning, proceed as for Blender Wheat Cakes.

Serves 2-3

CREPES and BLINTZES

Crepes are basically very thin pancakes that take no leavening. They are very versatile—they can be glazed, rolled, filled or wrapped around a slice of fruit.

Pastry wheat and oat flours make the most tender crepes. When frying up a batch, stack them gently in an ovenproof dish. Cover them with a tea towel to keep them warm for serving. If you are making several batches of crepes, keep the covered dish in a warming oven or main oven set on low temperature. Be careful. As crepes dry out, they get tough. A great part of the delight in eating these pancakes is their tenderness, their "melt-in-the-mouth" quality. A good crepe should be somewhat elastic.

There are any number of crepe pans on the market, which, while handy, are not necessary. I have always used two 8 inch cast iron skillets. (The 8 inch is the manufacturer's measurement from rim to rim; the bottom of the pan actually makes a 6 inch crepe.) Once seasoned, a cast iron pan offers steady, uniform heat and requires only a drop or two of oil or a pea sized piece of butter between crepes.

Crepes may sound like work, but in the long run they are a time saver. There is no need to separate the eggs. Moreover, the batter only improves while you tend to other morning chores. The crepes cook rapidly and the cast iron pans need only to be wiped clean. Any extras can be frozen and quickly thawed in the oven when you need them. They hold up well in storage, even in the refrigerator.

Since crepe batter must stand at least 15 minutes, and preferably an hour before cooking, I use instant non-fat milk powder instead of non-instant, as in stack pancakes. The longer standing time allows the milk granules to dissolve thoroughly, and I enjoy the sweeter flavor imparted by instant milk.

When I retested these recipes, I thought it might be more convenient to use whole fluid milk in place of water and milk powder. After numerous experiments, however, my husband and I both concluded that the best crepe was still the one made with instant milk powder and water.

Crepe Technique

If the pans are well-seasoned, there will be no need to oil them for the first crepe or two. If the pans appear dry, drop in a few drops of melted butter (or a pea sized lump) and swirl around. Holding the handle of one skillet at a time, ladle a small amount of batter in the center of the pan and swirl the pan around so that the batter just covers the bottom. After a few crepes, you will be able to judge just how much batter to put in. It is a fine line between too much batter and too little, but in either case, the crepe will still be edible. If you have not put in enough batter, quickly add more and swirl the pan. If you have poured in too much, resign yourself to a thick and indelicate crepe. Keep practicing your technique — mastery may only be a crepe away.

Cook the crepes over moderately high heat. When using two pans, you will be pouring and turning constantly, since the batter cooks quickly. As soon as the tops appear dry — 1 to 2 minutes — turn the crepe and let it cook in the skillet only long enough to brown the underside. Most of the cooking is done before turning. Run a metal spatula around the edges of the crepe to loosen it from the pan. The edges are always thin and may tend to stick to the sides of the pan where there is the least butter or oil. Then insert the spatula under the center of the crepe and turn. When the underside is brown (30 seconds to 1 minute) transfer the crepe to a warm dish or plate. Cover with a tea towel and tend to the rest of the batter.

Pastry crepes are complemented by any fruit sauce or filling. As with all crepes, spread a tablespoon or more of the filling on the flat crepe, then roll. The filling may be fruit, nut butter spread, yogurt, or grated cheese. The number of garnishes is limited only by your imagination. Date or maple sugar sprinkled on the crepe before rolling is often enough, but don't hesitate to add a drizzle of maple syrup and chopped nuts, even a dollop of whipped cream and fresh fruit.

Pastry Crepes

3/4 c. whole wheat pastry flour
1/8 tsp. salt
3 large eggs
1 c. water
1/2 c. powdered instant non-fat milk

1. In a medium bowl, measure and mix the pastry flour and salt.
2. In a small bowl, whisk together the eggs, water and milk powder.
3. Pour the liquid ingredients into the dry and beat thoroughly with a wire whisk. Cover the bowl (a luncheon plate usually works fine) and let stand from 15 minutes to an hour. This resting period gives the grain and milk powder time to absorb moisture and produces an even textured crepe. Stir again before cooking.
4. Heat a crepe pan or 2 to 3 cast iron skillets. The quantity of crepes will vary depending on the size of the skillets.

Yield: 18 to 20 thin pancakes

---————VARIATIONS————---

100% Barley Crepes

Follow the recipe for Pastry Crepes, using 3/4 cup barley flour (ground from whole barley in a steel mill) in place of the pastry wheat flour. Because barley is sweeter than wheat, it goes well with any fruit sauce.

100% Rye Crepes

Follow the recipe for Pastry Crepes, using 3/4 c. whole rye flour (ground from rye berries the same way you would grind wheat berries) in place of the pastry wheat flour.

100% Buckwheat Crepes

Follow the recipe for Pastry Crepes, but substitute buckwheat flour for the whole wheat pastry flour.

Oat Crepes

This wheat free pancake should be at the top of everyone's list for flavor, texture, high protein and low calories. A sweet crepe, it goes well with any fruit sauce filling or just plain bananas, sliced or mashed, drizzled with honey and topped with yogurt.

Follow the recipe for Pastry Crepes, using 3/4 cup of oat flour in place of the 3/4 cup pastry wheat flour.

Carob Crepes

Spoon 3 T. carob flour into a 1 cup measure. Fill to 3/4 level with pastry flour. Add 1/4 tsp. cinnamon. Good with maple syrup or carob sauce.

Snap Apple Crepes

Use 3/4 cup of apple juice in place of water and dry milk. Use extra large eggs in place of large eggs to get added elasticity.

Chunky Apple Crepes

Prepare the batter for Pastry Crepes, adding 1 T. maple syrup to the liquid ingredients. Just before pouring onto the griddle, stir in 1 medium apple, cored and finely chopped. Add a pea sized piece of butter to the skillet between crepes to make turning easier.

Brush with melted apple jelly or maple syrup and roll for serving.

Graham Crepes

These are called "Graham" as distinct from Pastry Crepes because they are made with hard wheat. The same amount of moisture handles less hard wheat than pastry flour, hence, the basic recipe is adjusted as follows.

Graham Crepes maintain the full bodied flavor of wheat, at its best when freshly ground and griddled.

> 2/3 c. whole wheat flour (hard)
> 1/8 tsp. salt
> 3 large eggs
> 1 c. water
> 1/2 c. powdered instant non-fat milk

1. Into a medium bowl, combine the flour and salt.
2. In a small bowl, measure and whisk together the eggs, water and milk powder.
3. Combine liquid and dry ingredients and whisk thoroughly. Cover and let stand 20 minutes to 1 hour.
4. Cook as for Pastry Crepes.

Yield: 18-20 crepes

―――――――――VARIATIONS―――――――――

Wheat Germ Crepes

The flavor of wheat germ seems to combine best with its natural companion, whole wheat flour.

Spoon 3 T. wheat germ into a 1 cup measure. Fill to 2/3 level with hard wheat flour. Proceed as for Graham Crepes.

Nut Crepes

To any basic crepe recipe, add up to 1/4 cup ground cashews, almonds or sesame seeds. Finely ground pecans, walnuts or macadamias can also be added in the same amount.

Blintzes

A blintz is a crepe filled with cheese or fruit and sauteed in butter. Any crepe can fill in for a blintz, but the standard against which all flavors are measured is the Pastry Crepe.

Make one batch of Pastry Crepes. This will yield 15 to 18 thin pancakes. Cool the cooked crepes before filling, or wait until the next day (refrigerate them overnight). Any crepes that have been filled, however, should be sauteed immediately, since the water in the filling will weep into the crepe unless the crepe is re-cooked. Leftover sauteed blintzes can be stored refrigerated and reheated the next day.

> 1 pound ricotta (2 cups)
> 2 T. honey
> 1 T. lemon juice
> 1 egg yolk

1. Combine the cheese, honey, lemon juice and egg yolk.
2. Place 2 to 3 tablespoons (depending on the size of the crepe) in the center of each pancake. Fold over the side edges as for an envelope, then roll.
3. Melt a tablespoon of butter in a medium sized skillet and saute the blintzes, seam side down, until golden, then turn and saute the other side. Repeat with the remaining blintzes.
4. Serve warm with Cinnamon Apple Compote and yogurt or sour cream. The recipe for the compote is on the following page.

Yield: 15-18 blintzes

Cinnamon Apple Compote

2 large apples (or 3 medium), peeled and cut into chunks
apple juice or water for cooking
1/3 c. honey
1/4 tsp. cinnamon

1. Place the apples in a medium saucepot.
2. Add just enough apple juice or water to start the apples cooking, and simmer slowly, covered, over low heat until the apples are softened.
3. Stir in the honey and cinnamon. Simmer for another 3 minutes so that the honey and cinnamon are well combined with the apples. If the cooked apples are especially juicy, thicken with a small amount of arrowroot dissolved in apple juice.
4. Serve warm or chilled.

GRANOLA SNACKS and BARS

Granola is basically a multi-ingredient cereal mixed for eating dry or with milk, yogurt or any other milk product, including nut and soy milks. Granolas are the ultimate challenge and delight of the cereal cook. The variables are endless: the grains can be floured, powdered or flaked; the nuts can be ground, shredded, chopped, roasted or raw; fruit can be added or omitted.

Oil and/or butter are added to the grains giving them, when baked, the desired crunch. At the same time, the moistening requires longer cooking time in the oven so that the cereal, which has absorbed the honey and fats, can roast under cover of this coating. When recipes simply call for dry roasting of the basic grains used in the granola mix without the addition of honey and butter, the resulting cereal will initially be crisp when the cereal is poured into a bowl, but it will quickly become soggy when milk is added. Honeyed and buttered grains, on the other hand, retain their crunch through to the last spoonful.

Individual preferences will ultimately influence each person's list of ingredients. Fruited granolas are very popular but require several precautions. If the dried fruits are added before the cereal flakes are toasted, they are likely to scorch unless the oven is set at an extremely low heat. Yet at such a low heat setting, perhaps 225 degrees F., the cereal flakes do not get very crispy, and the end product is a compromise. If the fruits are added after the rest of the ingredients have cooked and cooled, they tend to impart moisture to the roasted ingredients during storage and produce another equally compromised granola (unless you happen to prefer soft granola). For these reasons, I do not recommend adding fruit to the granola mix until the cereal is served, and then individual portions of dried raisins, chopped apricot, pineapple, papaya, or apple or any combination of fresh fruits can be added (especially bananas and fresh berries).

Cereal proteins should be complemented whenever possible

by the addition of other cereal grains, nuts, seeds, and milk. For those who must restrict intake of milk products, granolas make an attractive cereal choice, since the other ingredients can be proportioned for maximum protein. Wheat germ could be increased as well as seeds such as sunflower and pumpkin. Soy and sesame seeds are a good source of calcium, and so are almonds and brazil nuts, although to a lesser degree.

There is no market substitute for a homemade granola that has been prepared with fresh grains, plump seeds and fresh butter. Oats are traditionally a major component of granolas, but wheat and rye flakes alone or in combination make tasty cereals. Wheat germ for extra protein and bran for increased fiber are two important additions and can be adjusted according to individual needs. If you want less bran, simply replace it with a slightly larger amount of rolled oats. (The larger oat flakes have less surface area than an equal measure of the smaller bran particles, which is why you'll need slightly more oats for the same amount of liquid.) Sweeteners should come from the honey, maple syrup or molasses group to include trace minerals. The average ratio of liquid to dry for a crunchy cereal is 5 1/2 cups of dry ingredients to 1 cup liquid. Usually the liquid component is equally divided between the sweetener and the butter.

Stainless steel pans or cookie sheets should be used in baking because of all the turning involved in maintaining an evenly browned cereal. The granola should cover the entire sheet or pan to a depth of up to 1/2 inch. Do not crowd the pan, however, since this will make turning difficult. Bake the cereal at an oven temperature of 325° F. and check the trays at ten minute intervals. The edges will brown first, and it is necessary to lift the browned cereal with a metal spatula and move it to the center of the tray. The center portion should be gradually moved out toward the edges with each successive rotation of the cereal.

Baking time varies with ovens. Small ovens will brown the edges more quickly. Wood stoves tend to brown more evenly than electric. Gas stoves come closest to duplicating the effects of radiant wood heat. Whatever type of oven you have, be sure that the cereal is thoroughly dry when you remove it from the oven. This can be checked quickly by removing about one teaspoon of the cereal from the tray and allowing it to cool. Within a few minutes it will crisp if it is done cooking. There is no greater insult to the name of granola than sticky, not quite cooked oats. When the entire tray is golden, remove it from the oven, and let it cool completely on a wire or wooden rack before transferring to storage containers. Use lidded glass or plastic jars for keeping. The lids should be tightly fastened to keep the cereal from absorbing moisture from the air and losing its crunch. Glass and plastic are recommended over tin cans or containers since oily grains, nuts and seeds tend to go rancid quicker in tins than in glass or plastic. Unless the granola will be eaten on a regular basis and has been made in small batches, it is always a good idea to keep it refrigerated.

The controversy of oil versus butter in these recipes may be found in the Introduction. For health reasons, I have chosen to use butter.

Branola

This granola is a taste and texture favorite for snacking and granola bars. It can be eaten straight or with raisins, with or without milk. When spooned over a dish of yogurt and sliced bananas, it turns breakfast into dessert!

    1/2 c. butter, salted
    1/2 c. butter, unsalted
    1 c. honey*
    6 c. rolled oats
    2 c. miller's bran
    1 c. raw wheat germ
    1 c. raw hulled sunflower seeds
    1 c. coarsely chopped almonds
    1 c. unsweetened grated coconut
    1/4 c. raw unhulled sesame seeds

1. Heat the butters and honey over low flame until liquified.
2. In a large bowl combine the remaining ingredients.
3. Pour the honey/butter mixture over the dry ingredients and stir until all the dry ingredients are thoroughly moistened. Stir up from the bottom of the bowl to be sure that the liquid mixture has evenly coated the oats and nuts.
4. Spread this mixture onto four ungreased cookie sheets (or two batches of two cookie sheets) and bake at 325°F. for 25 to 35 minutes, depending on the type of oven. Keep turning and rotating the cereal at intervals as the edges brown. When the granola has turned uniformly golden, remove the cookie sheets from the oven and let the cereal cool on the trays before removing for storage.

Yield: 3 quarts

---

* If you're trying to cut down on honey, reduce the amount to 3/4 c. and add 1/4 c. unsweetened apple juice to the liquid ingredients.

Maple Pecan Granola

1/2 c. unsalted butter
1/2 c. salted butter
1 c. pure maple syrup
8 c. rolled oats
1 c. miller's bran
2 c. raw wheat germ
1 c. coarsely chopped or broken pecans
1 c. hulled sunflower seeds

1. Over low heat, melt the butters and maple syrup.
2. In a large bowl, combine the remaining ingredients.
3. Pour the liquid ingredients over the oat and seed mixture and stir with a wooden or stainless steel spoon until the dry ingredients are thoroughly and evenly moistened.
4. Spread the granola on ungreased stainless cookie sheets and bake at 350°F. for 30 minutes, or until evenly browned and crisp. Turn and rotate the cereal at 10 minute intervals and check an oat flake occasionally to see if the cereal is done.
5. Cool the granola on the trays, then remove with a spatula and transfer to glass or plastic containers for storage.

Yield: 3 quarts

Carob Granola

Brown rice flour milled by hand in a Corona or similar steel mill is grainy, like cornmeal, which is an ideal texture for a crunchy granola. Commercially milled rice flours, on the other hand, are often processed at high heat and the resulting product is extremely powdery and unsuitable for this recipe. If you don't have access to the right kind of rice flour, increase the oats.

The addition of milk powder to the carob and rice gives this granola a malted milk taste.

- 1/2 c. unsalted butter
- 1/2 c. salted butter
- 1 c. honey
- 1 c. brown rice flour
- 6 c. rolled oats
- 1 c. bran
- 1 c. raw wheat germ
- 2 c. powdered instant non-fat milk
- 2 c. coarsely chopped raw almonds
- 1 c. carob flour
- 1 c. unsweetened dried shredded coconut
- 1 tsp. cinnamon

1. Warm the butters and honey until liquefied.
2. Combine in a large bowl the remaining ingredients.
3. Pour the liquid ingredients over the dry and stir thoroughly, until the honey/butter mixture is evenly distributed throughout the mix.
4. Spread the granola on stainless steel cookie trays and bake at 325°F. for 20 to 30 minutes, or until lightly browned and crisp. This cereal must be watched carefully (at 5 to 7 minute intervals) because the milk powder and carob scorch easily. Turn and rotate the cereal frequently during baking.
5. Cool the granola on the trays, then remove with a spatula to storage containers.

Yield: 3 quarts

Gingerbread Granola

This is a good snacking cereal. It needs no additional milk to complement its protein and the distinctive taste is as habit forming as ginger snaps.

Wheat germ flour and bran form small nuggets of crisp gingerbread when coated with the molasses/honey mixture, and their protein is complemented by the sunflower seeds, milk powder and cashews. This is another case where the texture of hand milled grains is essential to the finished granola. The flour should be grainy. If you can get durum wheat flour, use it.

Serve with plenty of raisins.

1/2 c. honey
1/2 c. molasses
1/2 c. salted butter
1/2 c. unsalted butter
6 c. rolled oats
1 c. bran
1 c. raw wheat germ
1 c. hard wheat flour (bread or durum)
1 c. powdered instant non-fat milk
1 c. raw hulled sunflower seeds
1 c. chopped raw almonds, cashews or filberts
2 tsp. cinnamon
2 tsp. ginger

1. Warm until melted in a small saucepan the honey, molasses and butters.
2. In a large bowl, measure and combine the remaining ingredients.
3. Pour the warmed liquid ingredients over the dry mix and stir until it is thoroughly moistened.
4. Spread the granola on ungreased stainless cookie sheets and bake at 325°F. for 30 minutes, or until lightly browned. Turn and rotate the cereal as the edges brown, usually at 10 minute intervals.
5. Cool on the trays before serving.

Yield: 3 quarts

A Word on Wheat Germ

Although rolled oats and other cereal flakes are the usual main components in crunchy granolas, they are by no means the last word in toasted breakfast cereals. Wheat germ is a cereal in its own right with 12 grams of protein per half cup serving. It is an excellent source of potassium and phosphorus, B-1, B-2, and niacin.

Fresh wheat germ is pale gold in color and smells delicious. Make sure that the wheat germ you serve meets both of these qualifications, since rancid wheat germ is disagreeable to the taste buds and the digestive system. As a rich source of vitamin E and wheat germ oil, the flakes must be protected, through refrigeration, from oxidizing.

While wheat germ can be eaten raw, a light toasting improves the flavor without causing a serious loss of nutrients. Simply spread a thin layer of wheat germ in a stainless steel, glass or enamelware pan and toast in the oven for 5 to 7 minutes at 275°F. On top of the stove, in a dry cast iron skillet, the germ will take a little longer—7 to 10 minutes—over low heat with occasional stirring. The wheat germ can then be eaten with sliced fresh fruit, raisins, or fruit purees, such as applesauce or apricot puree. It can be sprinkled on yogurt or eaten as a regular cereal with milk.

Crunchy Wheat Germ

Enjoy this for breakfast or dessert with fresh fruit and cream or yogurt. The recipe may be doubled, tripled or quadrupled.

1 T. butter
1 T. honey
1/4 tsp. cinnamon
1 c. raw wheat germ

1. Melt the butter, honey and cinnamon in a pan.
2. Stir the liquids into the raw wheat germ and combine thoroughly with a wooden spoon. All the flakes should be uniformly coated.
3. Spread the moistened wheat germ on the bottom of an ungreased stainless or enamelware or glass pan and toast in a 325°F. oven for about 15 minutes. Check after 10 minutes to see if the edges need to be turned in toward the center.
4. At the end of the cooking time, the wheat germ will still seem moist, but it will crisp upon cooling. When it is thoroughly cooled, transfer it to a tightly lidded container, glass or plastic, and refrigerate.

Yield: a little over 1 cup

Wheat Germ Mixes

Regular Toasted or Crunchy Toasted Wheat Germ can be combined with any of the following ingredients, depending on individual preference.

> **seeds, raw or roasted (sunflower, pumpkin, chia, millet, sesame)**
> **roasted chopped peanuts**
> **chopped nuts, raw or roasted (pecans, almonds, cashews, walnuts, pine nuts, filberts, macadamias, pistachio, brazil, hickory)**
> **chopped dried fruits (dates, figs, raisins, pineapple, apricot, papaya, apple, banana)**

The above ingredients can be added directly to the toasted wheat germ and stored in a closed container with the cereal. Fresh fruits should be added to the cereal bowl when the wheat germ is served.

Wheat germ mixes make a compact breakfast that is good when a light, high protein cereal is desired. They can be eaten as a trail food or mixed with dairy, nut or soy milks and served in the conventional way. Layer the mix with yogurt or sprinkle it on top of yogurt that's on top of pancakes. Fold it inside crepes with a sauce.

The following two mixes are suggestions to give you an idea of the proportions to use when making up your own wheat germ mixes.

Crunchy Apricot Mix

1 c. Crunchy Wheat Germ
1/2 c. chopped dried apricots (moisturized or sulfured, so that they're reasonably soft)
1/4 c. dried shredded coconut
1/2 c. chopped raw cashews

1. Measure into a small bowl the Crunchy Wheat Germ, apricots, coconut and cashews.
2. Store, refrigerated, in a tightly lidded container.
3. See serving suggestions above.

Crunchy Date Mix

1 c. Crunchy Wheat Germ
1/2 c. chopped pitted dates
1/2 c. chopped raw almonds
1/4 c. chopped walnuts

1. Measure the ingredients into a small bowl and combine.
2. Store, refrigerated, in a tightly lidded container.
3. See serving suggestions above.

A Note on Granola Squares

Granola squares can be taken anywhere and eaten anywhere, without bowls or spoons. Made basically from cereal flakes, wheat germ, nuts, fruits and seeds, they are a bit bulkier than wheat germ bars per gram of protein, but they pack more fiber. All cereal flakes preserve the bran layer of the whole berry and additional wheat bran insures proper movement of food through the digestive system as well as a protection against pollutants. Persons allergic to wheat can substitute more rolled oats, rolled rye, nuts, or seeds for the high fiber (bran) component of wheat. Use soy, peanuts or seeds to substitute for the high protein (germ) component of wheat.

A boiled syrup of honey, molasses, maple syrup, sorghum or a combination of these does the best job of holding the dry ingredients together. For this reason, the flakes, nuts and seeds should be toasted without any liquid coating (in contrast to the way you coat and bake for granola). This can be done by measuring the dry ingredients into a 9 x 12 inch stainless or enamelware pan and baking them at 325°F. for 20 to 30 minutes. Wheat germ should be added to the pan for the last 10 minutes of toasting only. Check the grains and seeds occasionally and turn if the edges begin to brown.

While the dry ingredients are cooling, the syrup should be brought to a boil. It is not necessary to cool the dry components any longer than it takes to make the syrup, which should be poured over the dry ingredients immediately and stirred vigorously. It is essential to mix up these squares rapidly and transfer them to a buttered 8 x 8 inch pan before the syrup hardens.

The proportion of syrup to flakes and other additions varies slightly from that for regular granola. *Approximately 4 cups of dry ingredients requires 2/3 cup syrup.* Favorite granola recipes (unsweetened) can be mixed up, toasted plain, then turned into squares according to these proportions.

Coconut Squares

Two squares provide approximately 12 g. protein. Since coconut is relatively low in protein, I have used a larger proportion of wheat germ than in other recipes.

2 c. rolled oats
1/2 c. unsweetened dried shredded coconut
1/4 c. raw hulled sunflower seeds
1/4 c. chopped raw almonds
1/4 c. miller's bran
3/4 c. raw wheat germ
1/2 c. honey
3 T. butter
1/4 tsp. vanilla

1. Measure the oats, coconut, sunflower seeds, almonds and bran into a 9 x 12 inch baking pan and toast at 325°F. for 20 minutes.
2. Add the wheat germ and toast for an additional 10 minutes.
3. Place the honey and butter in a small saucepan. Bring to a boil then reduce the heat and continue to boil for 5 minutes, stirring to prevent scorching.
4. Add the vanilla, then pour the hot honey/butter over the dry ingredients. Stir quickly and thoroughly to make sure that all ingredients are coated.
5. Transfer the hot mixed cereal to a lightly buttered 8 x 8 inch pan. Let cool 1 to 2 minutes, then press down firmly with buttered palms.
6. When the cereal is room temperature, cut with a sharp serrated knife into 9 squares. Transfer to a storage container or wrap in clear plastic and refrigerate.

Yield: 9 squares

Maple Squares

Two squares provide 13 grams of protein.

- 2 c. rolled oats
- 1/2 c. chopped raw cashews
- 1/4 c. raw hulled sunflower seeds
- 1/4 c. chopped raw pecans
- 1/4 c. miller's bran
- 1/2 c. raw wheat germ
- 1/4 c. honey
- 1/4 c. maple syrup
- 3 T. butter
- 1/4 tsp. vanilla

1. Measure the oats, cashews, sunflower seeds, pecans and bran into a stainless or enamelware pan (9 x 12 inch) and bake for 20 minutes at 325°F.
2. Add the wheat germ and toast an additional 10 minutes. Transfer these ingredients to a medium sized bowl and prepare the syrup.
3. Spoon the honey into a half-cup measure. Fill to the top with maple syrup. Pour the honey/maple syrup into a small saucepan. Add the butter.
4. Bring the liquids to a full rolling boil, reduce heat and boil for 5 to 7 minutes, stirring occasionally to keep the syrup from scorching. Add the vanilla just before pouring over the dry ingredients.
5. Pour the boiling syrup over the toasted grains and stir rapidly to coat the oats and nuts thoroughly.
6. Transfer the coated mix into a lightly buttered 8 x 8 inch pan. Let cool 1 to 2 minutes, then press firmly with buttered palms. When the pan is room temperature, cut into 9 squares.
7. Wrap the squares in clear plastic wrap or store in a tightly lidded glass or plastic container and refrigerate.

Yield: 9 squares

Cinnamon Apple Squares

Two squares provide approximately 16 1/2 grams of protein. High fiber sesame seeds take the place of additional bran in this recipe.

2 1/2 c. rolled oats
1/2 c. raw unhulled sesame seeds
1/2 c. raw hulled sunflower seeds
1/3 c. wheat germ
1/2 c. chopped dried apple
1/2 tsp. cinnamon
1/2 c. raw unfiltered honey
3 T. butter

1. Toast the oats, sesame and sunflower seeds in an ungreased 9 x 12 inch pan for 20 minutes at 325°F.
2. Add the wheat germ and toast for an additional 10 minutes.
3. While these ingredients are toasting, place the dried apple into a medium sized bowl. Add the toasted ingredients plus the cinnamon and stir until well mixed.
4. Prepare the syrup by placing into a small saucepan the honey and butter. Bring these to a full boil over medium heat; reduce heat and keep at a full boil for 5 minutes, stirring to avoid scorching. Pour the liquid over the dry ingredients, stirring rapidly to coat the oats/seeds/apple mixture evenly. Transfer to a lightly buttered 8 x 8 inch pan and let cool 1 to 2 minutes. Then press down firmly into the bottom of the pan.
6. When the mixture is room temperature and has hardened, cut into 9 squares with a sharp knife. Store in a lidded container or individually wrapped portions. Refrigerate.

Yield: 9 squares

Branola Squares

Portable packages of everyone's favorite — Branola.

1 1/2 c. rolled oats
1/2 c. miller's bran
1/2 c. raw hulled sunflower seeds
1/2 c. chopped raw almonds
1/2 c. unsweetened dried shredded coconut
2 T. raw unhulled sesame seeds
1/2 c. raw wheat germ
1/2 c. honey
3 T. butter

1. In a 9 x 12 inch baking pan, measure and mix the oats, bran, sunflower seeds, almonds, coconut, and sesame seeds. Bake at 325°F. for 20 minutes.
2. Add the wheat germ and bake an additional 10 minutes. Transfer the toasted ingredients to a medium sized bowl.
3. Measure the honey and butter into a small saucepan and bring to a boil. Reduce heat and boil gently, for 5 minutes.
4. Pour over the toasted ingredients and stir until the honey/butter has coated the branola mix.
5. Transfer the coated cereal to a lightly buttered 8 x 8 inch pan. Cool slightly then press down into the pan as firmly as possible.
6. Cool to room temperature, then cut into 16 squares. Refrigerate, either in the pan, covered, or wrapped in individual portions.

Yield: 16 squares

Wheat Germ Bars

Wheat Germ Bars are a compact alternate to Granola Squares. Wheat germ, the basic ingredient, is a densely packed source of protein and takes up little space compared with the nutrition it offers.

One cup of wheat germ supplies: Protein, 22 g.; Fiber, 2 g.; Thiamin (B-1), 1.6 mg.; Riboflavin (B-2), .56 mg; Niacin, 3.4 mg.; Potassium, 680 mg.; Phosphorus, 920 mg.; Iron, 7.7 mg.

1 1/2 c. plain raw wheat germ
1 1/2 to 2 c. mixed chopped nuts or seeds
1/2 to 3/4 c. chopped roasted peanuts
1/2 c. chopped dried fruit*
1/2 c. honey
3 T. butter

Toast the wheat germ. This can be done on top of the stove in a heavy skillet or in the oven. In the skillet, stir the wheat germ over moderate heat until golden, between 5 and 10 minutes. In the oven, spread a thin layer in a baking dish and toast at 275°F. for 5 to 7 minutes. Add the remaining ingredients.

The total should be 3 3/4 c. of wheat germ and finely chopped nuts, seeds and fruits. Make a syrup by bringing the honey and butter to a boil. Boil hard for 5 minutes, then pour the syrup over the dry ingredients and stir until they are thoroughly coated. Press into a lightly buttered 8 x 8 inch pan, cool 5 minutes, and press again. After 15 minutes, cut with a sharp knife.

Yield: 15 bars

---

* Use moisturized packs of apricots, peaches, and pears, as they are too leathery if *totally* dried (moisture free). Timber Crest's Sonoma label is the best brand of moisturized fruit on the market. In contrast, raisins, dates, figs, apples and prunes usually retain enough moisture without extra "moisturizing" to make them chewy.

Sesame Apple Bars

Each bar contains approximately 6 grams of protein. The sesame seeds are an excellent source of calcium, phosphorus and potassium. Cashews provide the same three nutrients, plus vitamin A. The apples are high in potassium.

> 1 1/2 c. plain toasted wheat germ
> 3/4 c. chopped dried apple
> 3/4 c. lightly toasted unhulled sesame seeds
> 3/4 c. finely chopped raw cashews
> 1/4 tsp. cinnamon
> 1/2 c. honey
> 3 T. butter

Follow directions as in Wheat Germ Bars.

To toast sesame seeds, spread a 1/4 inch layer in the bottom of a heavy gauge pan and set over low heat. Stir occasionally for 5 to 10 minutes, or until a few seeds begin to pop and they have turned slightly golden. Toasting brings out the full sesame flavor.

Yield: 15 bars

Peanut Apple Bars

Peanuts and sunflower seeds complement each other to provide over 7 grams of protein per bar.

> 1 1/2 c. plain toasted wheat germ
> 3/4 c. chopped roasted peanuts
> 3/4 c. raw hulled sunflower seeds
> 3/4 c. finely chopped dried apple
> 1/2 c. honey
> 3 T. butter

1. In a medium sized bowl, combine the wheat germ, peanuts, sunflower seeds and apple.
2. Place the honey and butter in a small saucepan. Bring to a full rolling boil and boil for 5 minutes, stirring constantly to prevent scorching.
3. Pour the boiling liquid over the dry ingredients, stirring rapidly to distribute the honey and butter evenly over the wheat germ and nuts.
4. Transfer the mixture to a lightly buttered 8 x 8 inch pan and press down firmly with the back of a stainless steel spoon or spatula. Cool for 5 minutes and press again with buttered palms, compacting the bars as much as possible.
5. Let cool an additional 5 minutes, then cut into 15 bars. When the bars are cool, wrap in clear plastic or in tightly lidded containers and refrigerate.

Yield: 15 bars

DESSERTS

  If I had to choose a single recipe out of this cookbook to bake for someone who had never eaten anything made from whole grains, I would probably be able to please that person most easily with a dessert.
  If you use soft wheat flour (there is no substitute for it in desserts) and a very mild honey (Peace River White Clover from Canada is the finest, if you can find it), I guarantee that you can pack any of these cookies and cupcakes into lunchboxes with confidence that they will be enjoyed.

Pie Crust and Pastry Dough

This is an extremely simple recipe that will serve you in good stead for all of your pies, tarts, turnovers and pastry crust needs. It is tender and tastes good; no one would ever suspect that it's whole wheat. The dough is easy to work and coheres well; you have no need to fear a crumbly whole wheat crust.

> **1 c. plus 1 T. whole wheat pastry flour**
> **1/8 tsp. salt**
> **1/4 c. melted butter**
> **2 1/2 to 3 T. water**

1. If you're making pie crust, measure the flour and salt directly into the pie pan.
2. Emulsify the melted butter and 2 1/2 T. water and stir into the flour/salt with a fork until well-combined. If it is not cohering well, add 1/2 T. more water. Remember whether your flour takes 2 1/2 or 3 T. water for making crusts in the future.
3. Gather the dough into a ball. At this stage you can either pat it out into the pan or roll it between two sheets of waxed paper for an absolutely uniform crust.
4. Use as you would any pie crust. For double crusted pies, simply double the recipe, cut in half and roll out each half between waxed paper.

Yield: 1 pie crust

Apple Pan Dowdy

An old time apple dessert; the spicing has a mincemeat flair.

1 1/2 T. whole wheat pastry flour
1 tsp. cinnamon
1/4 tsp. cloves
1/4 tsp. nutmeg
1/4 c. molasses
1/4 c. honey
8 c. sliced apples
1/2 c. dark raisins
1/2 c. coarsely chopped walnuts

1. In a medium large bowl, combine the flour, cinnamon, cloves, nutmeg, molasses and honey.
2. Stir in the apples, raisins and walnuts.
3. Pack the apple mixture into a shallow (approximately 2 inches deep) buttered 1 1/2 quart baking dish.
4. Cover the apple mixture with a top crust. Use the preceding pie crust recipe. Drape the rolled dough over the dish, trim to about one-half inch excess all around and tuck in around the edge.
5. Bake 45 minutes at 400°F.

Serves 4

Apple Cobbler

Serve this hot out of the oven. Spoon out servings into individual dishes, inverting each portion so that the apples are on top. Add a scoop of vanilla ice cream or pour over fresh heavy cream.

>   7 c. sliced tart apples
>   1/2 c. honey
>   1/8 to 1/4 tsp. salt
>   1/2 tsp. cinnamon
>   several dashes nutmeg
>   1 c. whole wheat pastry flour
>   1 1/2 tsp. baking powder
>   1/8 tsp. salt
>   1/4 tsp. whole milk
>   2 T. melted butter
>   1 T. honey
>   1 egg

1. In a medium pot combine the apples, honey, salt and spices. Cover, bring to a boil over medium heat, reduce heat and simmer until the apples are softened and the honey syrup is thickened. Keep warm.
2. Prepare the cobbler topping by combining the flour, baking powder and 1/8 tsp. salt in a small bowl.
3. In a cup or small dish emulsify (with a fork) the milk, melted butter, honey and egg. Pour this mixture all at once into the flour mixture and stir with a fork until well-combined.
4. Transfer the hot apple mixture to a buttered glass 8 x 8 baking dish. Top with the cobbler batter and bake about 25 minutes at 400°F. The cobbler topping should be golden and the apple mixture will be bubbling madly about the edges. Allow to settle down before serving.

Serves 4

Lemon Yogurt Pie

A beautiful tangy pie that holds its sculptured shape in the refrigerator (in the unlikely event that you have any leftover).

1 pre-baked whole wheat pie crust
1 pkg. plain gelatin
1/4 c. cold water
1/2 c. honey
1/4 c. lemon juice (approximately the juice of one-half lemon)
8 ounces cream cheese, softened
1 tsp. freshly grated lemon rind
1 c. plain yogurt

1. Dissolve the gelatin in water.
2. Over medium heat, warm the honey and lemon juice. Stir in the gelatin until completely dissolved. Chill this mixture until syrupy.
3. Beat the cream cheese until fluffy. Beat in the lemon rind, then the congealing gelatin mixture.
4. In a separate bowl, beat the yogurt until smooth, then fold it into the gelatin/cream cheese mixture.
5. Allow this filling to chill slightly (do not allow to set) then mound into the pre-baked pie shell. Return to the refrigerator to set completely before serving (a few hours should be enough).

Serves 4-6

Pumpkin Pie

An updated version of the pumpkin pie that's been in everyone's recipe file for years. This time try it with honey for a mellow feast.

>2 eggs
>1 16 oz. can pumpkin
>2/3 c. honey
>1/8 tsp. salt
>1 tsp. cinnamon
>1/2 tsp. ginger
>1/4 tsp. cloves
>1 13 oz. can evaporated whole milk
>1 unbaked 9 inch whole wheat pie shell

1. In a medium bowl, whisk together, in order, the eggs, pumpkin, honey, salt, cinnamon, ginger, cloves and evaporated milk.
2. Pour the pumpkin mixture into an unbaked 9 inch whole wheat pastry crust.
3. Bake 15 minutes at 400°F., then reduce heat to 350°F. and bake an additional 45 minutes.

Serves 4

Pecan Pie

If you enjoy pecan pie (or tarts for that matter) but could do without the corn syrup, treat yourself to this affordably rich version.

1/4 c. butter
1 tsp. vanilla
3 eggs
1/3 c. honey
1/3 c. maple syrup
3 T. water
1 1/2 c. chopped pecans
1 unbaked whole wheat pie crust

1. Beat the butter until fluffy.
2. Beat in the vanilla, eggs, honey, maple syrup and water, in order.
3. Stir in the pecans.
4. Pour the mixture into an unbaked pie shell and bake 30 minutes at 350°F.

Serves 6

Vanilla Cream Pie

1 pre-baked whole wheat pie crust
1/4 c. honey
2 T. maple syrup
2 T. arrowroot powder
2 T. whole wheat pastry flour
2 whole eggs
2 c. whole milk
1 tsp. vanilla
1 T. butter

1. In a medium saucepan combine the honey, maple syrup, arrowroot, flour, eggs and milk.
2. Cook over medium heat, whisking or stirring constantly until the mixture just boils. Remove from heat and stir in the vanilla and butter.
3. Cool the filling before you add it to the pre-baked pie crust. This filling may also be used for cream puffs.

Serves 4

---VARIATIONS---

Coconut Cream Pie

Add 1/2 c. dried shredded coconut to the cream filling while still hot. When cool, transfer into a baked pie crust and top with 1/4 c. toasted shredded coconut.

Almond Cream Pie

Add 1/2 tsp. almond extract in addition to 1 tsp. vanilla to the cooked filling. Transfer the cooled cooked filling to a baked pie shell and top with chopped toasted almonds.

Banana Cream Pie

In a baked pie crust, alternately layer the cooled filling with thinly sliced bananas. Top with whipped cream, if desired.

Impossible Pie

This is the same impossible pie you've heard of, the one that makes its own crust, only this time it's made impossibly better by using wholesome ingredients.

    4 large eggs
    1/2 c. soft honey
    2 c. milk
    1/2 c. whole wheat pastry flour
    1/4 c. melted butter
    1 tsp. vanilla
    1 c. dried shredded coconut

1. In a medium bowl, whisk together in order, the eggs, honey, milk, flour, melted butter and vanilla.
2. Stir in the coconut.
3. Pour the mixture into a buttered 9 inch glass pie dish and bake 35 to 40 minutes at 350°F., or until a knife inserted 2 inches from the edge comes out clean. Cool or chill before serving.

Serves 4

Cream Puffs

Cream puffs always look so elegant yet are so easy to make. With whole wheat pastry flour you can serve light and tender puffs with good conscience.

> 1 c. whole wheat pastry flour
> 1/8 tsp. salt
> 1/2 c. butter
> 1 c. whole milk
> 1 tsp. honey
> 4 eggs

1. Be sure to have all ingredients at room temperature. Measure the flour into a small bowl and combine with the salt. Set aside.
2. In a medium saucepot, bring the butter, milk and honey to a boil. Add the flour mixture all at once and stir rapidly with a wooden spoon until smooth and the dough leaves the sides of the pot. Remove from the heat and let stand 2 minutes.
3. Again using a wooden spoon, beat in the eggs one at a time. The dough will look slippery after the addition of each egg, but beat vigorously until it is thoroughly blended before adding the next egg.
4. Let the dough stand while buttering a cookie sheet. Spoon the batter into small mounds or shapes (allowing room to expand).
5. Bake at 400°F. for 10 minutes, reduce heat to 350°F. and continue baking for another 25 minutes. No peeking!
6. Cool the shells thoroughly before filling. See recipes for Cream Pie Fillings on pages 150-151 or Bakery Style Cream Filling, page 158.

Carob, Date and Nut Loaf

A moist and chocolatey loaf that freezes well. I use Pero, a German coffee substitute made from a mixture of roasted grains to give the batter a rich hue, although you may use instant coffee just as well.

1 c. coarsely chopped walnuts
1 c. chopped pitted dates
1 c. boiling water
7/8 c. honey
1/3 c. melted butter
2 beaten eggs
1/2 c. carob flour
1/4 tsp. Pero or instant coffee (for dark "fudge" color)
1 tsp. vanilla
1 3/4 c. whole wheat flour (hard)*
1 tsp. baking soda
1 tsp. cinnamon
1/4 tsp. salt

1. Place the nuts and dates in a small bowl. Pour the boiling water over them and allow to cool.
2. Meanwhile, combine, in a medium bowl, the honey, butter, eggs, carob flour, Pero and vanilla.
3. In a separate bowl, combine the hard wheat flour, baking soda, cinnamon, and salt.
4. Drain the water from the dates and nuts when it has cooled and reserve. There should be approximately 1/2 cup. If less, add water to equal 1/2 cup and mix this liquid alternately with the flour to the honey/butter/egg mixture.
5. Butter two small loaf pans (7 3/8 x 3 5/8 x 2 1/4) and line the two long sides and bottom of each with a single sheet of waxed paper or cooking parchment. Butter the waxed paper and ends of the pans (or if using parchment, just the ends of the pans). This will make the loaves easy to remove from the pans. Pour in the

batter and bake at 350°F. for 30 minutes, or until a toothpick inserted in the centers comes out clean.

6. To remove the loaves from the pans after 20 minutes of cooling, loosen the short ends of the pans with a knife, then grasp the two exposed edges of paper and pull out gently. Cool thoroughly on wire racks before wrapping and storing.

Yield: 2 small loaves

* Be sure to use *hard* wheat flour; the proportion of liquids is too high for pastry flour.

Hot Water Gingerbread

1/2 c. melted unsalted butter
1 tsp. cinnamon
1 tsp. ginger
1/2 tsp. cloves
1/2 tsp. baking soda
7/8 c. molasses
1 egg
1/4 tsp. salt
2 1/4 c. hard wheat flour
1 1/2 tsp. baking powder
1 c. hot water

1. In a medium bowl, whisk, in order, the melted butter, cinnamon, ginger, cloves, soda, molasses, egg, and salt.
2. Combine the flour and baking powder in a small bowl, then whisk the mixture into the spiced liquids alternately with the hot water.
3. Pour the batter into a buttered 9 x 9 inch pan and bake 35 minutes at 350°F.

Yield: 1 square gingerbread

Boston Gingerbread

2 c. whole wheat pastry flour
1 tsp. cinnamon
1 tsp. ginger
1/2 tsp. nutmeg
1/4 tsp. salt
1 tsp. soda
1/2 c. molasses
1/4 c. honey
1/2 c. butter
2 eggs
1/2 c. plain yogurt

1. Combine the flour, spices, salt and soda in a medium bowl.
2. Melt the molasses, honey and butter and let cool.
3. Whisk the eggs into the molasses mixture.
4. Add the flour alternately with the yogurt (pre-stirred) to the liquid ingredients.
5. Pour the batter into a well-buttered 9 x 9 inch pan and bake 30 minutes at 375°F.

Yield: 1 square loaf

———————VARIATIONS———————

Apple Gingerbread

Use 1/2 c. apple juice in place of yogurt, and stir in 1/2 c. coarse walnuts before baking.

Orange Gingerbread

Use 1/2 c. orange juice in place of yogurt, and stir 1 to 2 tsp. grated orange rind into the batter.

Spice Cupcakes

1/4 c. butter
1/3 c. honey
1 egg
1 c. whole wheat pastry flour
1/2 tsp. baking soda
1/8 tsp. salt
1/2 tsp. cinnamon
1/4 tsp. each clove and nutmeg
1/3 c. plain yogurt

1. Cream the butter and honey in a medium bowl.
2. Beat in the egg.
3. Measure and stir the flour, baking soda, salt and spices. Add this mixture to the creamed ingredients alternately with the yogurt.
4. Spoon the batter into 8 large (or 12 small) buttered muffin cups and bake 18 minutes at 375°F. Use Vanilla Cream Cheese Frosting, page 160.

Yield: 8-12 cupcakes

Carob Cake / Cupcakes

The same recipe will work for a single 9 x 9 inch cake, two 8 inch layers or 18 medium cupcakes.

1/2 c. butter
2/3 c. room temperature honey
1 tsp. vanilla
2 whole eggs
1 3/4 c. whole wheat pastry flour
1 tsp. baking soda
1/3 c. carob powder
1/4 tsp. salt
1/2 tsp. cinnamon
2/3 c. plain yogurt (pre-stirred until smooth)

1. Cream the butter and honey until light and fluffy. Beat in the vanilla and eggs.
2. In a small bowl, measure and combine the flour, baking soda, carob flour, salt, and cinnamon.
3. Using a mixer at low speed or beating by hand, add the flour alternately with the yogurt in three portions.
4. Pour the batter into a buttered and floured 9 x 9 or 7 x 11 pan and bake at 350°F. for 40 to 45 minutes, or until a toothpick inserted in the center comes out clean. (Bake 8 inch layers for 20 to 25 minutes at 350°F., and cupcakes 20 minutes at 375°F.)

Yield: 1 loaf or 18 cupcakes

Vanilla Cream Cheese Frosting

4 ounces cream cheese
2 T. honey
1/4 tsp. vanilla
1 to 2 tsp. milk

1. Beat the cream cheese until fluffy.
2. Beat in the honey and vanilla.
3. Add the milk a drop at a time, beating constantly, until the frosting is very light. Do not add the milk too quickly or too much milk; the frosting will lose its air and become runny.

Yield: frosting for 12 small cupcakes

Boiled Honey Frosting

This is one honey frosting that's guaranteed to hold its shape, in refrigerator or out, for days. It's a beautiful fluffy white frosting that complements any cake. Combine it with whipped heavy cream for a heavenly bakery style cream puff filling (see Cream Puff recipe).

1/2 c. honey
1 large egg white
1/8 tsp. salt
1/2 tsp. vanilla

1. In a small saucepan, bring the honey to a boil.
2. Beat the egg white until stiff in a medium bowl. Add the salt, then add the boiling honey in a slow steady stream. Beat continuously for several minutes, until the frosting thickens.
3. Add the vanilla and continue beating until the frosting holds its shape and becomes difficult to beat any further (it should be the consistency of marshmallow cream).
4. Use immediately or store in the refrigerator for later use.

Yield: frosting for a 9 x 9 inch cake

---------- VARIATION ----------

Bakery Style Cream Filling

Prepare Boiled Honey Frosting using 1 egg white, and divide the mixture in half, reserving half for another use. Whip 1 cup heavy cream until stiff and gradually fold in the measured boiled honey frosting.

Yogurt Cheesecake I

This makes a large unbeatable New York Style cheesecake; it's an adaptation of my mother's recipe, known and published for many years simply as Helma's Cheesecake. Plain yogurt makes a lighter cheesecake than the original sour cream but it's still rich rich rich.

1 pound cottage cheese
1 pound cream cheese
1 c. honey
4 beaten eggs
1 T. lemon juice
1 T. vanilla
1/4 c. whole wheat pastry flour
1/4 c. arrowroot powder
1/2 c. butter, melted
2 c. plain yogurt

1. Sieve the cottage cheese or blend until smooth. Sieving gives the cheese the particular texture that's become associated with New York Style cakes, but it's quite delectable made with cottage cheese processed in the blender until smooth.
2. Cream the cream cheese and honey, then whisk in the sieved cottage cheese.
3. Add the beaten eggs, incorporating thoroughly, then whisk in the lemon juice and vanilla.
4. Whisk, in order, making sure to blend well after each addition, the flour, arrowroot, melted butter and yogurt.
5. Pour the batter into an ungreased 10 inch springform pan. Bake 1 hour at 350°F., turn the oven off (without peeking!) and leave the cake in the oven for 2 more hours. Remove from the oven, loosen and remove the springform, and chill the cake before eating.

Yield: 1 10-inch cake

Yogurt Cheesecake II

This recipe makes a "Sara Lee" style cheesecake with a shortbread crust and sour cream topping. Made lighter by using plain yogurt for part of the cream, it's still a dessert for special occasions.

1/4 c. butter
1 T. honey
3/4 c. whole wheat pastry flour
1 pound cream cheese
1/3 c. honey
3 eggs
2 tsp. lemon juice
1 c. plain yogurt
1 c. sour cream
2 T. honey
1 tsp. vanilla
1/4 c. finely chopped walnuts
cinnamon

1. To prepare the crust, cream the butter and one tablespoon honey, then stir in the flour. Pat the shortbread into an 8 or 9 inch springform pan, bringing it up 1 1/4 inches on the 8 inch pan, 1 inch up the sides of the 9 inch pan. If you have trouble getting the crust to adhere to the pan, butter it lightly.
2. Prebake the crust for 15 minutes at 350°F., then cool.
3. In a medium bowl, whisk, in order, the softened cream cheese, honey, beaten eggs, lemon juice and yogurt. Pour into the cooled crust and bake 30 minutes at 350°F., then 30 minutes more at 325°F. Remove from the oven and let cool one half hour.
4. In a small bowl, whisk together the sour cream, two tablespoons honey and vanilla. Pour over the cheesecake, sprinkle with the nuts and cinnamon, then bake 10 minutes at 350°F.
5. Remove from the oven and cool to room temperature before removing the springform and chill at least 6 hours before serving.

Basic Baked Custard

This low fat recipe will make a four serving bowl of custard that supplies 13.5 g. protein per serving. Powdered milk insures a perfectly set custard every time, although you may use whole milk in place of water and milk powder or a combination of milk and cream for a richer dessert.

4 eggs
1/4 c. honey
2 c. water (room temperature)
1 c. powdered instant non-fat milk
1/8 tsp. salt
1/2 tsp. vanilla
pinch nutmeg

1. In a medium bowl, beat the eggs.
2. Beat in the honey, water, milk, salt and vanilla.
3. Pour the mixture into an ungreased glass 1 quart baking dish and sprinkle with nutmeg.
4. Place the baking dish in a pan of hot water and set the pan in a 325°F oven. The pan of hot water insures a smooth texture. (Custard left to its own devices in the oven may toughen). Bake for 40 to 50 minutes or until set. A knife inserted an inch from the edge of the custard will come out clean if the custard is done baking.
5. Cool slightly and serve warm (or chilled) with granola, crunchy wheat germ, or just plain.

Serves 4

VARIATIONS

Rice Custard

A high fiber (rice bran) custard that is equally rich in protein, zinc, calcium, potassium and iron.

>**Basic Baked Custard recipe**
>**2 c. cooked brown rice**
>**1/4 c. chopped pitted dates**
>**1/4 c. coarsely chopped walnuts, cashews or whole hulled sunflower seeds**
>**dash cinnamon**

1. Before baking stir into the Basic Baked Custard the rice, dates and walnuts.
2. Sprinkle with cinnamon and bake the custard at 350°F. in a 1 1/2 quart glass baking dish that has been set in a pan of hot water. Check the custard after 45 minutes with a knife to see if it is set.

Serves 6

Maple Custard

Use 1/4 c. maple syrup instead of honey in the Basic Baked Custard recipe. Serve with melted raspberry jam or jelly glaze.

Crumb Custard

Eggs, milk and whole grains — it's all there in one dish. This is truly a custard, although bread or cake crumbs baked in an egg/milk matrix are usually called puddings.

> 4 leftover muffins or 4 whole wheat rolls
> 2 c. water*
> 1 c. powdered instant non-fat milk
> 4 eggs
> 1/4 c. honey
> 1/2 tsp. vanilla
> 1/4 tsp. cinnamon
> 1/4 c. raisins
> 1/4 c. raw hulled sunflower seeds

1. Dice or crumb 4 muffins or rolls and place in a buttered 1 1/2 quart baking dish (glass).
2. Mix the water and milk. Pour over the muffins or rolls.
3. Beat together the eggs, honey, vanilla and cinnamon. Pour over the soaked crumbs and toss lightly with a fork.
4. Toss in the raisins and sunflower seeds.
5. Place the crumb custard dish in a baking pan filled with approximately 1 inch of hot water and place in a 350°F. oven for 45 minutes. Insert a knife near the edge of the bowl to see if the custard is done.
6. Serve warm or chilled.

Serves 6

* For a richer custard, you may use 2 cups whole milk instead of water and milk powder.

Crisp Oat Chippers

A versatile oatmeal cookie that stays crisp.

1 c. butter
1/2 c. honey
1 tsp. vanilla
1/8 tsp. salt
2 c. whole wheat pastry flour
1 c. rolled oats
1 c. carob chips
1/2 c. chopped walnuts

1. In a medium bowl, cream the butter, honey, vanilla and salt.
2. Add, stirring in order, the flour, oats, carob chips, and walnuts.
3. Chill the dough at least 1 to 2 hours. Longer is fine. Roll into balls, then flatten with a fork on lightly buttered cookie trays.
4. Bake 15 to 20 minutes or until golden, at 325°F. Transfer to wire racks to cool thoroughly before storing.

Yield: 3-4 dozen cookies

———————VARIATIONS———————

Raisin Oatmeal Cookies

Use 1 c. raisins in place of carob chips and add 3/4 tsp. cinnamon, 1/4 tsp. clove, and 1/4 tsp. allspice to the flour.

Coconut Orange Cookies

Use 1/2 c. coconut in place of the carob chips and add 1 to 2 tsp. freshly grated orange rind and 1/4 tsp. allspice to the creamed ingredients. Use pecans instead of walnuts.

Cashew Date Cookies

Mixed grains, milk protein and fruits combine to make these cookies more than just a sweet treat.

2 1/2 c. hard wheat flour
2 c. rolled oats
1 1/2 c. raw broken cashews
1 c. raisins
1 c. chopped pitted dates
1 1/2 tsp. cinnamon
1 tsp. allspice
1 tsp. baking soda
1/4 tsp. salt
1 c. honey
3/4 c. melted butter
2 eggs
1/2 c. milk
1 1/2 tsp. vanilla

1. In a large bowl measure and combine the flour, oats, cashews, raisins, dates, cinnamon, allspice, baking soda and salt.
2. In a medium bowl cream together the honey and butter, then whisk in the eggs, milk, and vanilla.
3. Pour the liquid ingredients into the dry and let stand while heating the oven to 350°F. to allow the grains to soak up moisture. Drop by the rounded teaspoon onto buttered cookie trays and bake 10 minutes, or until the centers spring back when pressed lightly. Remove to racks to cool.

Yield: 6 1/2 dozen cookies

Poor Man's Cookies

When these cookies were first invented (probably during Depression days), they were made with pantry staples — solid shortening, white flour and sugar — hence the name. Made with whole wheat and fortified with wheat germs, raisins and walnuts, there's no longer anything poor about them.

2/3 c. honey
1/2 c. butter
1 c. raisins
3/4 c. water
1 tsp. cinnamon
1 tsp. cloves
2 c. hard wheat flour
1/2 c. raw wheat germ
1 tsp. baking soda
1/2 c. chopped walnuts

1. Boil together for 5 minutes the honey, butter, raisins, water, cinnamon and cloves.
2. When cool, stir in a mixture of the flour, wheat germ, and baking soda. Stir in the nuts.
3. Chill the batter, then drop onto buttered cookie sheets by the well-rounded teaspoon. Bake 12 minutes at 350°F. or just until the centers spring back when lightly touched. Do not overbake.

Yield: 3 1/2 dozen cookies

Old Fashioned Ginger Snaps

These really snap — very gingery.

2/3 c. molasses
6 T. butter
2 c. whole wheat pastry flour
1/2 c. wheat germ
2 tsp. ginger
1/2 tsp. soda

1. Bring to a boil the molasses and butter. Cool.
2. Combine the remaining ingredients and add to the liquid ingredients. Mix thoroughly.
3. Chill until almost frozen, then roll out on a lightly floured surface (working with only a portion of the dough at a time) until 1/4 inch thick. Cut out 2 inch rounds. Bake 10 minutes at 350°F. on buttered cookie sheets. Transfer to wire racks to cool. They will get crisp as they cool.

Yield: 4 dozen cookies

Coconut Macaroons

These are incredibly easy to make. Be sure to use parchment paper for flawless macaroons.

2 c. dried unsweetened finely shredded coconut (sometimes called "macaroon" coconut)
1/3 c. soft honey
3 egg whites
1/2 tsp. vanilla
1/2 tsp. almond extract
pinch salt

1. Place the coconut in a small bowl. Combine it with the honey, stirring with a fork.
2. Stir in the unbeaten egg whites, vanilla, almond extract and salt.
3. Place a piece of cooking parchment on a cookie tray. Form the coconut mixture into small round shapes with your hands (a bit over an inch in diameter and about 1/4 inch thick) and place on the parchment. If you prefer, you can shape the macaroons in more of a haystack fashion off the tip of a teaspoon.
4. Bake the macaroons for 20 to 22 minutes at 325°F. or until golden. Remove from the parchment and place on wire racks to cool. They should lift off easily from the paper.

Yield: 36 macaroons

Date Bars

There are date bars and there are date bars, most of them based on an egg and flour dough. These, combining oats, wheat and coconut, are simply heaven. Organically grown dates make the richest tasting filling that needs no vanilla to fill out the flavor. Unlike the dark sticky pasteurized dates sold in regular supermarkets, naturally dried dates are tawny colored and easy to pit. Simply slice each date in half, remove the pit with the tip of a knife, then cut the halves into 3 or 4 pieces to form chunks.

    2 c. chopped pitted dates
    3/4 c. water
    1/2 c. chopped walnuts
    1 1/2 c. rolled oats
    1 c. whole wheat flour (hard)
    1/2 c. dried shredded coconut
    1/3 c. melted butter
    1/3 c. honey

1. Simmer the dates and water over low heat until the dates have softened and form a spreadable paste, about 5 minutes. Stir in the walnuts.
2. While the date mixture is cooling, combine the oats, flour and coconut.
3. Warm the butter and honey sufficiently to just melt the butter, then stir this mixture into the flour/oat/coconut mixture with a fork until the dry ingredients are uniformly moistened. Spread half of this crust mixture into the bottom of an 8 x 8 inch pan and press down firmly.
4. Spread the date/walnut mixture evenly over the bottom crust.
5. Sprinkle the remaining crust mixture over the top of the dates and press down gently. Bake at 350°F. for 35 to 40 minutes, or until the top is browned. Cool thoroughly, then cut into bars with a sharp knife.

Yield: 12 bars

Date and Nut Squares

This, unlike the preceding recipe, is based on an egg and flour dough, barely sweetened.

> 2 eggs
> 2 T. honey
> 1/2 tsp. vanilla
> 1/2 c. whole wheat pastry flour
> 1/2 tsp. baking powder
> 1/8 tsp. salt
> 2 c. chopped pitted dates (natural and moist)
> 1 c. coarsely chopped pecans or walnuts

1. In a medium bowl, whisk, in order, the eggs, honey and vanilla.
2. Measure, in a separate bowl, the flour, baking powder, and salt.
3. Whisk the flour mixture into the eggs/honey until smooth. Stir in the dates and nuts.
4. Spread the batter into a buttered 8 x 8 inch or 9 x 9 inch pan and bake 25 minutes at 350°F.

Yield: 12 bars

Carob Brownies

2 eggs
1/2 c. honey
1/2 c. peanut butter
1 tsp. vanilla
1/4 c. carob powder
1/3 c. melted butter
1/2 c. whole wheat pastry flour
1/2 tsp. baking powder
1/4 tsp. salt
1/2 c. chopped walnuts or pecans

1. In a medium bowl, whisk together the eggs, honey, peanut butter and vanilla.
2. In a small bowl, whisk together the carob powder and melted butter, then add this to the eggs/honey mixture.
3. Combine the flour, baking powder and salt and add to the liquid ingredients. Stir in the chopped nuts.
4. Spread the batter in a buttered 8 x 8 inch or 9 x 9 inch pan and bake 25 minutes at 350°F.

Yield: 12 bars

Fig Newtons

1/2 lb. Calimyrna figs
1/4 c. water
2 tsp. butter
dash salt
1/4 c. butter
2 T. honey
1 egg
1/2 tsp. vanilla
1 1/4 c. whole wheat pastry flour
1/8 tsp. salt

1. Prepare the fig filling by cutting the stems off the figs and grinding (a meat grinder works great). Cook the figs with the water over low heat until soft. Add the 2 tsp. butter and dash of salt and then let cool.
2. Cream the quarter cup butter and honey. Beat in the egg and vanilla.
3. Stir in the flour and salt.
4. Spread half the batter in a buttered 8 x 8 inch baking dish, spread the filling on top, then cover with the rest of the batter. Bake 25 to 30 minutes at 350°F. until golden brown.

Yield: 12 bars

Lemon Almond Squares

The clean taste of lemon in three layers: a shortbread crust, lemon sponge and toasted almond garnish.

1/4 c. butter
2 T. honey
1/4 tsp. almond extract
3/4 c. whole wheat pastry flour
1/8 tsp. baking powder
1/4 c. ground raw almonds*
1/3 c. honey
2 large eggs
2 T. lemon juice
1/4 c. ground toasted almonds**

1. Cream the butter and 2 T. honey, then stir in the almond extract, flour and baking powder and ground raw almonds.
2. Press this mixture into a buttered 8 x 8 inch pan and bake 15 minutes at 350°F.
3. Meanwhile, prepare the lemon layer by whisking the third cup honey, eggs and lemon juice.
4. Pour the lemon mixture over the partially baked crust, return to the oven and bake 20 minutes longer. Remove from the oven and sprinkle the ground toasted almonds over the top.
5. Cool, then cut into squares.

Yield: 12 squares

* To grind raw almonds, simply process in the blender at the grind setting until fine.
** Toast ground raw almonds in a small dish or pan in a 350°F oven for 10 minutes. This can be done along with the lemon squares during the last 10 minutes of baking.

Apricot Cookie Bars

1/2 c. dried apricots
1/2 c. hot water
1/4 c. honey
1/3 c. butter
1/4 c. honey
1 c. whole wheat pastry flour
1 c. rolled oats
1/8 tsp. salt
1/2 c. chopped pecans

1. Pour one half cup warm water over the dried apricots and soak overnight.
2. In the morning, bring the apricots and liquid to a boil and simmer, covered, until soft. Puree in a blender with 1/4 c. honey. Set aside to cool.
3. Cream the butter and 1/4 cup honey. Stir in the flour, oats, and salt. Chill several hours or until firm.
4. Pat 2/3 of the dough into a buttered 8 x 8 inch pan. Stir the nuts into the apricot puree and spread this filling evenly over the bottom crust. Crumb the remainder of the dough on top and press lightly.
5. Bake 30 minutes at 350°F. or until golden.

Yield: 12 squares

Cashew Almond Confections

1 1/4 c. coarsely chopped raw almonds
1 1/4 c. coarsely chopped raw cashews
1/2 c. raw hulled sunflower seeds
1/2 c. honey
3 T. butter

1. Measure the nuts and seeds into a medium bowl.
2. In a medium saucepan, bring the honey and butter to a boil, reduce heat and boil for 5 minutes.
3. Stir the nuts and seeds into the hot honey butter mixture until well-coated, then remove from the heat. Transfer the mixture to a buttered 8 x 8 inch pan and press. When almost cool, cut into 18 bars.
4. For a nougat-like confection, boil the honey for 3 minutes, stir in the nuts and seeds and continue to stir over low heat for another 3 minutes.

Yield: 18 bars

Peanut Booster Bars

2 c. roasted peanuts, split
1 c. lightly roasted unhulled sesame seeds
1/2 c. honey
3 T. butter

1. In a medium bowl combine the peanuts and sesame seeds.
2. In a medium saucepan bring the honey and butter to a boil, reduce heat and boil for 5 minutes. Stir in the peanuts and seeds until well-coated, then transfer to a buttered 8 x 8 inch pan and press. Cool slightly, then cut into bars.

Yield: 18 bars

Sesame Squares

Crunchy, buttery squares of sesame brittle made entirely from honey, butter and seeds.

> 1 c. unhulled sesame seeds
> 1/4 c. butter
> 1/4 c. honey

1. Toast the sesame seeds either in a heavy skillet over moderate heat or in the oven. In the skillet, stir the seeds until lightly browned. In the oven, place the seeds in a pie pan or 8 x 8 inch baking pan and toast for 15 minutes at 350°F., shaking the pan every 5 minutes to redistribute the seeds. When golden, they are done.
2. In a medium skillet, melt the butter and honey. Bring to a boil and cook over moderate heat for 3 minutes.
3. Add the toasted sesame seeds and continue stirring over moderate heat for 2 to 3 minutes, or until the mixture begins to turn color.
4. Spread into a buttered 8 x 8 inch pan and cool before cutting into squares. Do not allow to harden completely before cutting.

Yield: 18 bars

Nut Butter Balls

Confections made from peanut and sesame butters offer the most protein. Sesame balls taste like halvah, and the cashew and almond butter confections can be addictive.

> 1/2 c. any nut butter — peanut, sesame, almond or cashew
> 2 T. honey
> 3 T. powdered instant non-fat milk

1. Stir all ingredients together. Knead briefly, then form into 16 inch sized balls. Roll in lightly toasted sesame seeds or leave plain. Allow to stand 20 minutes or more for the milk powder to dissolve.
2. Store refrigerated.

Yield: 16 balls

Carob Nut Balls

> 1/2 c. peanut butter
> 2 T. honey
> 2 T. powdered instant non-fat milk
> 1 T. carob powder

1. Stir together all ingredients. Knead briefly and roll into balls. Let them stand for a few minutes for the milk powder to dissolve. The dough is not sticky and does not require rolling in anything, but finely chopped nuts or coconut add contrasting flavor and texture.
2. For extra fudgy carob balls, omit milk powder and combine 1/2 c. peanut butter with 2 T. honey and 2 T. carob powder.

Yield: 16 balls

Index

Almond Cream Pie, 131
Almond Squares, 176
Apple Bars, 140, 142
Apple Cobbler, 146
Apple Compote, 122
Apple Crepes, 119
Apple Gingerbread, 157
Apple Pan Dowdy, 145
Apple Square, 137
Applejacks, 101
Apricot Cookie Bars, 177

Bagels, 32-33
Baked Custard, 164-166
Bakery Style Cream Filling, 161
Banana Bread, 71
Banana Cream Pie, 131
Barley Bread, 28
Barley Crepes, 117
Barley Muffins, 57
Bars, 172-177
Basic Graham Muffins, 55
Basic Pastry Muffins, 56
Basic Sweet Whole Wheat Yeast Dough, 20
biscuits, 46-52
Blender Bran Cakes, 111
Blender Corn Cakes, 113
Blender Nutty Wheat Cakes, 112
Blender Oat Cakes, 114
blender pancakes, 109-114
Blender Wheat Cakes, 110
Blender Wheat Oat Cakes, 111
Blintzes, 121-122
Blueberry Muffins, 59
Blueberry Pancakes, 102
Boiled Honey Frosting, 161
Boston Brown Bread, 76
Boston Gingerbread, 157
Bran Muffins, 68
Bran Cakes, 111
Branola, 126
Branola Squares, 138
breads, quick, 73-76
breads, yeasted, 27-29, 34-36
breads, yeasted, sweet, 20-26
Brown Bread, 76
Bubble Ring, 24
Buckwheat Bread, 28

Buckwheat Cakes, 101
Buckwheat Crepes, 118
Buckwheat Muffins, 58
buns, 37-45
butter vs. oil in baking, 14-15

cakes, 154-157, 159, 162-163
candies, 178-180
Carob Brownies, 174
Carob Cake, 159
Carob Crepes, 118
Carob Cupcakes, 159
Carob Date Nut Loaf, 154-155
Carob Granola, 128
Carob Muffins, 71
Carob Nut Balls, 180
Carrot Buns, 45
Carrot Pancakes, 103
Cashew Almond Confections, 178
Cashew Date Cookies, 168
Challah, 29
Cheddar Spoon Bread, 93
Cheese Crisps, 82
Cheese Kolaches, 26
Cheese Pone, 91
Cheese Scones, 52
cheesecakes, 162-163
Chunky Apple Crepes, 119
Cinnamon Apple Compote, 122
Cinnamon Apple Squares, 137
Cinnamon Buns, 26
Clover Leaves, 22
cobbler topping, 51
Coconut Cream Pie, 131
Coconut Macaroons, 171
Coconut Orange Cookies, 167
Coconut Squares, 135
Compote, 122
cookware, 10
Corn Bread, 28
Corn Bread, Yeasted, 36
Corn Cakes, 104, 113
Corn Fritters, 89
Corn Muffins, 58, 64
Corn Pecan Fritters, 88
Corn Pone, 91
Corn Tortillas, 85
crackers, 77-84
crackers, methods of rolling, 79-80

Cream Cheese Frosting, 160
Cream Pie Fillings, 130-131, 161
Cream Puffs, 153
crepe technique, 116
crepes, 115-120
Crescents, 22
Crisp Oat Chippers, 167
Crumb Cake Muffins, 61
Crumb Custard, 166
Crumb Topping, 61
Crunchy Apricot Mix, 133
Crunchy Date Mix, 133
Crunchy Wheat Germ, 131
cupcakes, 158-159
custards, 164-166
Cut Buns, 22

Date Bars, 172
Date Mix, 133
Date Nut Loaf, 154-155
Date Nut Squares, 173
Date Nut Muffins, 59
delayed kneading technique, 20
Dilled Carrot Buns, 45
dry milk, see milk

Eggless Muffins, 61
English Muffins, 30-31

Fig Newtons, 175
filling for cream pie, 130-131
filling for cream puffs, 130-131
Flaky Whole Wheat Biscuits, 46
flat breads, see tortillas
free radicals, 9, 14
French Toast, 96
fritters, 88-90
frostings, 160-161
Fruit Juice Muffins, 59
Fruit Kolaches, 26
Fruit Rolls, 94

Ginger Snaps, 170
Gingerbread, 156-157
Gingerbread Granola, 129
Gingerbread Muffins, 70
Graham Crepes, 120
Graham Muffins, 55
grain mills, 16-17
granola, 123-129
granola bars, 134-139
Granola Squares, 134
griddle cakes, 97-114

hard wheat, 11
Hard Wheat Flour Biscuits, 47

Herb Rolls, 42
Herbed Biscuits, 47
Herbed Rice Fritters, 90
Honey Drop Scones, 50-51
Honey Frosting, 161
Hot Cross Buns, 38-39
Hot Water Gingerbread, 156

Impossible Pie, 152
Irish Soda Wedges, 48

kneading dough, 19
kolaches, 26

Lemond Almond Squares, 176
Lemon Yogurt Pie, 147

Maple Custard, 165
Maple Pecan Granola, 127
Maple Pecan Muffins, 62
Maple Pecan Snails, 23
Maple Squares, 136
milk, dry vs. fresh, 12
  non-instant dry milk, 12-13
  instant, 12-13
Mixed Grain Thins, 81
muffins, 30, 53-72

Nut Butter Balls, 180
Nut Crepes, 120

Oat Bread, 28
Oat Cakes, 107, 114
Oat Cookies, 167
Oat Crepes, 118
Oat Flake Muffins, 67
oil, cooking, 14-15
Old Fashioned Ginger Snaps, 170
100% Barley Crepes, 117
100% Barley Muffins, 57
100% Buckwheat Muffins, 58
100% Corn Muffins, 58
100% Rice Muffins, 58
100% Rye Crepes, 118
Onion Rolls, 43
Orange Bread, 74
Orange Cookies, 167

pancakes, see griddle cakes
pasta machine, 79
Pastry Crepes, 117
pastry dough, 144
Pastry Muffins, 56
Peanut Apple Bars, 142
Peanut Booster Bars, 178
Peanut Butter Muffins, 63
Pecan Bread, 28

Pecan Granola, 127
Pecan Muffins, 62
Pecan Pie, 149
Pecan Snails, 23
pie crust, 144
pies, 144-152
Pineapple Sauce, 95
Pone, 91
Poor Man's Cookies, 169
Potato Buns, 44
Puffed Fruit Rolls, 94
Pumpernickel Bread, 34-35
Pumpkin Biscuits, 49
Pumpkin Bread, 74
Pumpkin Dinner Rolls, 41
Pumpkin Pancakes, 103
Pumpkin Pie, 148
Pumpkin Yeast Buns, 40

quick breads, see breads, quick
Quick Corn Fritters, 89

Raisin Bread, 28
Raisin Cinnamon Buns, 26
Raisin Oatmeal Cookies, 167
rancid foods, 3-9
red pastry wheat, 11
Rice Bread, 65
Rice Cakes, 101
Rice Custard, 165
Rice Fritters, 90
Rice Muffins, 58, 65
rolling crackers, 79-80
rolls, see buns
Rye Bread, 28
Rye Crackers, 83
Rye Crepes, 118
Rye Rolls, 43

scones, 48, 50-52
Sesame Apple Bars, 14
Sesame Squares, 179
shaping yeast dough, 22
shopping for ingredients, 8-9
Snap Apple Crepes, 119
soapstone griddle, 10
Soda Crackers, 84
soft wheat, 11
Soft Wheat Cakes, 100
Spice Cupcakes, 158
Spiced Muffins, 60
Spiced Pumpkin Yeast Buns, 40
Spiced Rye Muffins, 69
Spoon Bread, 92-93

Stollen, 25
Sweet Corn Pone, 91

Triticale Bread, 28
tortillas, 85-86
types of whole wheat, 11

Vanilla Cream Cheese Frosting, 160
Vanilla Cream Pie, 150

wheat germ, 130
wheat germ bars, 139-142
Wheat Germ Bars, 139
Wheat Germ Biscuits, 47
Wheat Germ Crepes, 120
wheat germ mixes, 130-133
Wheat Germ Muffins, 57, 66
Wheat Germ Yeast Pancakes, 107
Wheat Griddlecakes, 98-99
wheatless muffins, 57
white soft wheat, 11
Whole Wheat Bagels, 32-33
Whole Wheat Bread, 27
whole wheat flours, 11
Whole Wheat Sesame Thins, 78
   With Milk, 81
Whole Wheat Tortilla Shells, 86
Whole Wheat Yeast Pancakes, 106-107

Yeast Crackers, 83
yeast dough, sweet, 20-26
Yeast Muffins, 71
yeast pancakes, 106-108
Yeasted Buckwheat Cakes, 108
Yeasted Cornmeal Bread, 36
Yogurt Cheesecake, I and II, 162-163
Yogurt Pie, 147
Yogurt Wheat Germ Muffins, 66

Other Titles In The Crossing Cookbook Series

SWEET AND NATURAL, Desserts Without Sugar, Honey, Molasses or Artificial Sweeteners
by Janet Warrington
    Endorsed by the American Diabetic Association, this cookbook is a boon for families with a member suffering from diabetes.
$7.95

THE MAGIC MOUNTAIN DESSERT BOOK
by Debi Fischer
    This collection of prize desserts uses honey and molasses for sweetening, no white sugar. This is high gourmet baking of the natural food variety.
$7.95

WINGS OF LIFE, Vegetarian Cookery
by Julie Jordan
    This is a classic, 60,000 in print, many people swear by. The bread sections alone are worth the price of the book.
$7.95

ELEGANT EATING IN HARD TIMES, 59 Vegetarian Main Dishes
by Gloria Withim
    Complete menus for the fervent as well as the sometime-vegetarian.
$4.95

THE SPICE BOX, Vegetarian Indian Cookbook
by Manju Shivraj Singh
    Singh is Indian, trained as a home economist. The recipes are easy for a westerner to follow.
$7.95

SALADS OF INDIA
by Varsha Dandekar
    Dandekar is also Indian—the recipes are very lucidly presented, and the salads are knockouts in color and taste.
$4.95

You can get these books from your local bookstore or directly from The Crossing Press, Box 640, Trumansburg, N.Y. 14886. When ordering from us, please send check or money order and add $1.00 postage.